DIGITAL
landscape photography

A step-by-step guide to creating perfect photos

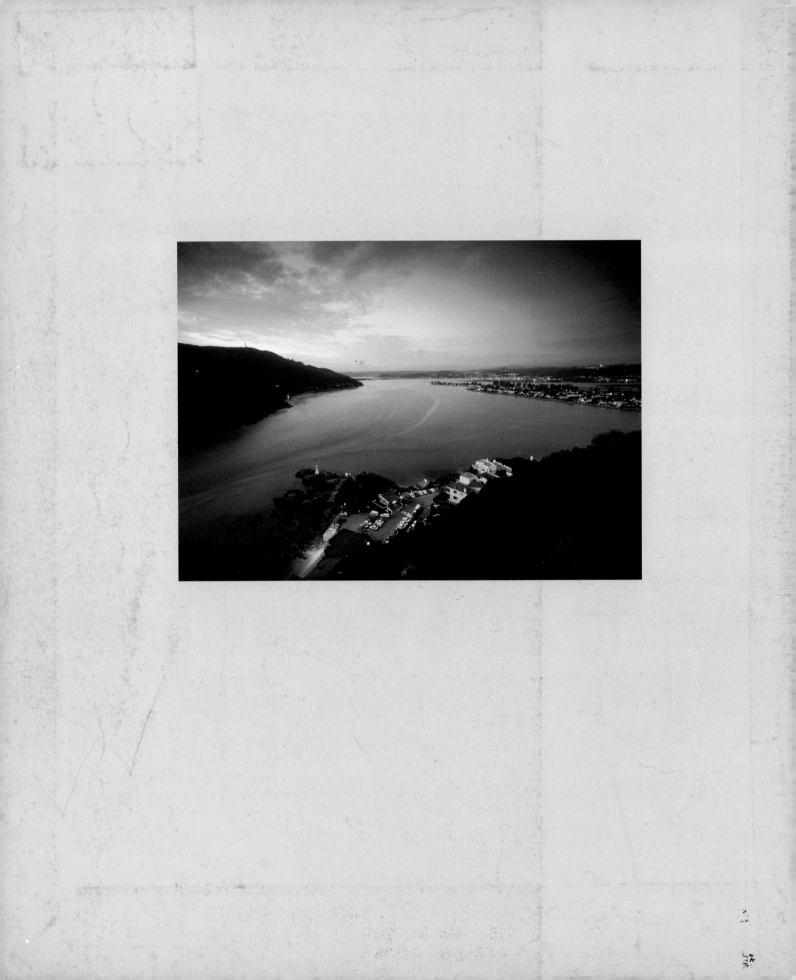

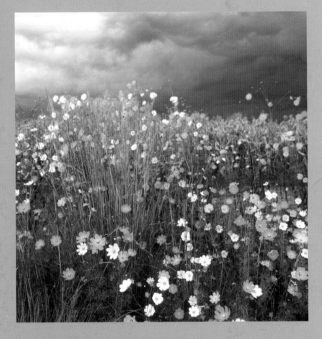

DIGITAL
➡ landscape photography

A step-by-step guide to creating perfect photos

TIM GARTSIDE

MUSKA&LIPMAN
Publishing

For Muska & Lipman Publishing:
Publisher: Stacy L. Hiquet
Senior Marketing Manager: Sarah O'Donnell
Marketing Manager: Heather Hurley
Associate Marketing Manager: Kristin Eisenzopf
Senior Aquisitions Editor: Kevin Harreld
Manager of Editorial Services: Heather Talbot
Senior Editor: Mark Garvey
Retail Market Coordinator: Sarah Dubois

ISBN 1-59200-107-6

5 4 3 2 1

Library of Congress Card Catalog Number 2003108397

Educational facilities, companies, and organizations interested in multiple copies or licensing of this book should contact the publisher for quantity discount information. Training manuals, CD-ROMs, and portions of this book are also available individually or can be tailored for specific needs.

MUSKA & LIPMAN PUBLISHING,
a Division of Course Technology
(www.course.com)
25 Thomson Place
Boston, MA 02210

www.muskalipman.com
publisher@muskalipman.com

This book was conceived, designed, and produced by
ILEX
The Barn, College Farm
1 West End, Whittlesford
Cambridge CB2 4LX
England

Sales Office:
The Old Candlemakers
West Street
Lewes
East Sussex BN7 2NZ
England

Publisher: Alastair Campbell
Executive Publisher: Sophie Collins
Creative Director: Peter Bridgewater
Editorial Director: Steve Luck
Series Editor: Stuart Andrews
Editor: Ian Probert
Design Manager: Tony Seddon
Designer: Jane Lanaway
Development Art Director: Graham Davis
Technical Art Editor: Nicholas Rowland

Printed in China

For more information on this title please visit:
www.sslaus.web-linked.com

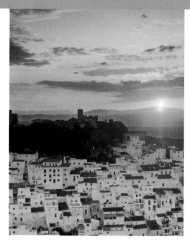

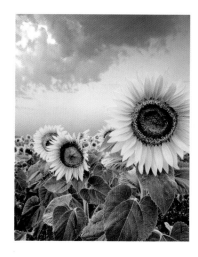

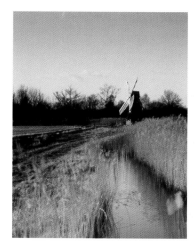

Contents

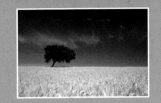
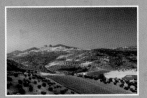

Introduction

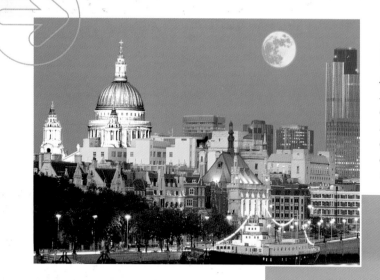

A telephoto lens was used to zoom in on London's St Paul's Cathedral and a tripod helped keep the image sharp over the eight-second exposure. The moon was added later.

The colors of this shot are not manipulated. Night scenes come alive with color as all the different light sources blaze away. Tungsten creates a warm glow, while mercury vapor lights create an eerie green. Use these colors to your advantage rather than trying to correct and change them.

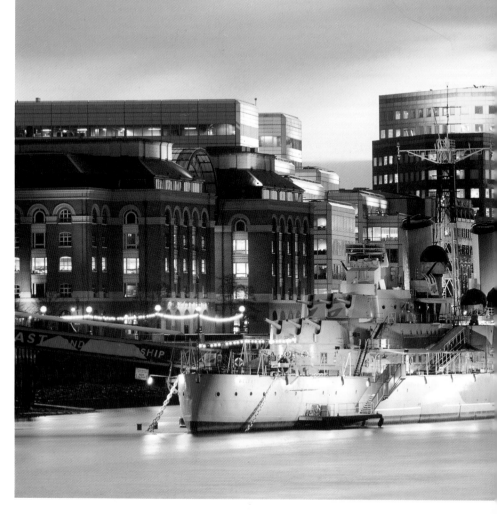

Taking a photograph is the end product of an emotional journey. Quite often, however, the final result is disappointing when compared to the memories of the original experience. Human vision is vastly superior to that of a camera lens and CCD. Along with visual memory, we also store emotional feelings about the moment—this is something that is a long way off with digital cameras! It is impossible to relay the full impact of the original moment because a print is two-dimensional, flat, without depth and emotion. We can, however, use the picture as a reminder, and the more powerful the image, the greater the stimulation we will feel. If you can learn to maximize the quality of your prints, then you can also maximize their emotional impact.

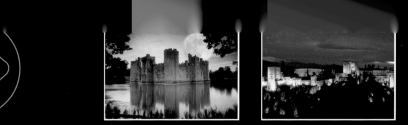

Bodiam Castle, England, was shot at dusk and the image was brightened on the computer. The full moon was added to the picture later. The sky in the shot of the Alhambra, Spain was also brightened to enhance the dramatic effect.

Human vision is much wider than a camera lens. This is because we are able to easily move our head and eyes around to create a 360° panoramic image. This is also part of the reason why a print fails—it simply cannot recreate the full image that we remember. With the stitching together of multiple shots we can now come closer to the impact of the original scene. Perhaps one day a digital camera will produce a 360° image that can be projected onto a screen in a small room to truly relive the moment.

The invention of photography was supposed to usher in the demise of fine-art painting: centuries of customs wiped out overnight. Of course, this was the opinion of a small minority of doom-and-gloom merchants getting all upset about nothing. In fact, this new medium created a fresh and exciting avenue for artists to explore. The doom-and-gloom merchants are back, however, claiming that digital photography will destroy traditional film photography as we know it.

As with most new technologies, there is an initial resistance and reluctance to embrace and learn digital photography. We are a suspicious lot and on the whole most of us don't like change, as with it comes the need to learn new methods. It is an inevitable fact now that digital cameras and pro digital backs will replace analog film cameras as the medium on which to capture images. How quickly this will happen is difficult to predict, but the big push will come when price and quality equal or improve upon traditional film cameras. I predict a niche market will always be there for film—especially black-and-white fine-art prints, which will become more sought as prized pieces of photographic art in galleries.

Years ago, as a photographer in the reprographic business, I was fortunate enough to recognize the creative potential of digital image manipulation. It was, however, some time before I could afford to purchase my own computer system. In the early days, computer systems would cost hundreds of thousands of dollars and need several huge magnetic tapes on which to store the digital information required for one image. These systems were housed in huge air-conditioned rooms. Nowadays, however, a digital system is more affordable and the average hard drive can store many times the capacity that roomfuls of digital tapes used to hold. Technology increases and cost decreases—both are advantageous to us, the consumer.

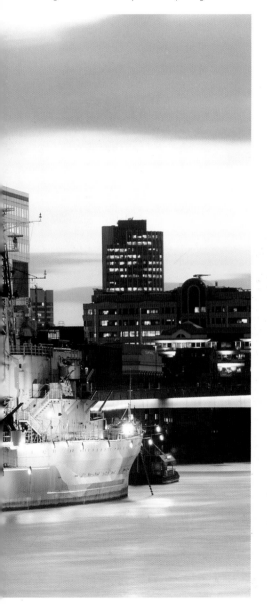

As a stormy day drew to a close I was waiting for some fireworks in the color of the sky. I was certainly not disappointed on this occasion. Stormy weather that clears in time can create some great skies for photography. The texture, shape, and color of these clouds add to the drama of the subject, especially when reflected in the river.

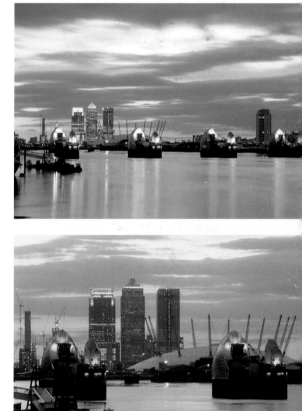

Using a zoom lens has let me create and combine several interpretations of this river scene by varying the focal length and changing the composition over time. I shot the scene over a 30-minute period, shooting as the ambient daylight changed and a sunset glow faded into evening dusk.

Introduction

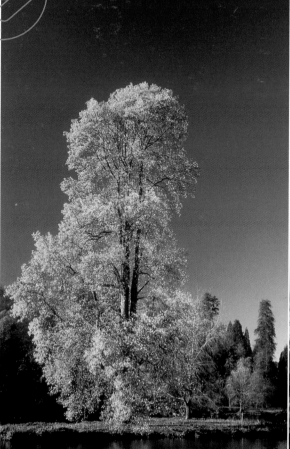

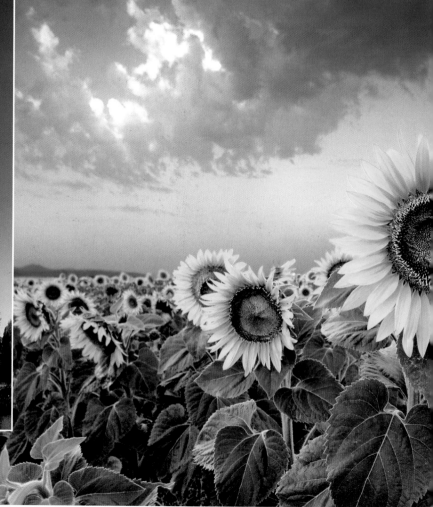

Capture the rich colors and splendor of the fall. Zoom in to emphasize one stunning tree and use a polarizer for intense colors.

These brilliant sunflowers were brightened up and the sky enhanced, to give a vibrant, colorful image. Careful selection of the sky with the Lasso tool was essential to maintain a realistic look.

The upside of digital photography is that you don't need film—in theory you should save money in the long run. This will depend on the cost of the camera and all the peripherals required to create an image. Another major advantage of digital photography is that it is instantaneous—you can view within seconds what you've just shot. To do this traditionally requires Polaroid film, which is horrendously expensive. The main disadvantage of downloading large files onto a memory stick or mini hard drive is the cost of the memory, although it is constantly falling in price.

Storage capacity is also getting better and smaller in size, which will be necessary as image files increase in size.

Power consumption is another problem that is being resolved as power supplies become smaller and last longer.

The chief hurdle to overcome is that to get the most out of your digital images you will need to learn how to manipulate them on a computer. The main advantage of using a computer is that you don't need a smelly darkroom or one-hour lab to do your image manipulation. You can do it in the comfort of

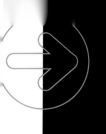

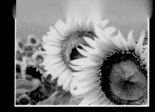

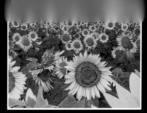

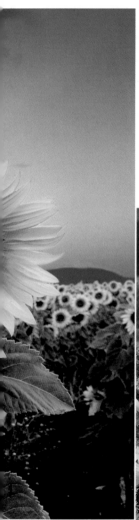

your own home or, if you have a laptop, just about anywhere you fancy. The digital darkroom is clean, warm, comfortable, bright, and you don't need to convert your bathroom into a darkroom any more!

Digital gives you more control over your images than ever before. You can produce prints that the best print labs would be proud of and even create prints that to produce traditionally would be very expensive or even impossible. In this book I shall be discussing all the traditional photographic techniques you

will need, such as cropping, color correction, tonal adjustments, dodging, and burning, as well as digital techniques such as using filters, sharpening, and using layers to create montages. All the techniques you require to create a masterpiece that you can proudly hang on the wall.

Future digital image-makers will blend together photographic reality with painting and illustration in order to create a new art form that combines the best features of both worlds.

These flowers were taken from several different angles, all shot at the same location under the same lighting. This is important for a coherent and homogenous effect. A sunlit sunflower would stick out like a sore thumb.

Introduction

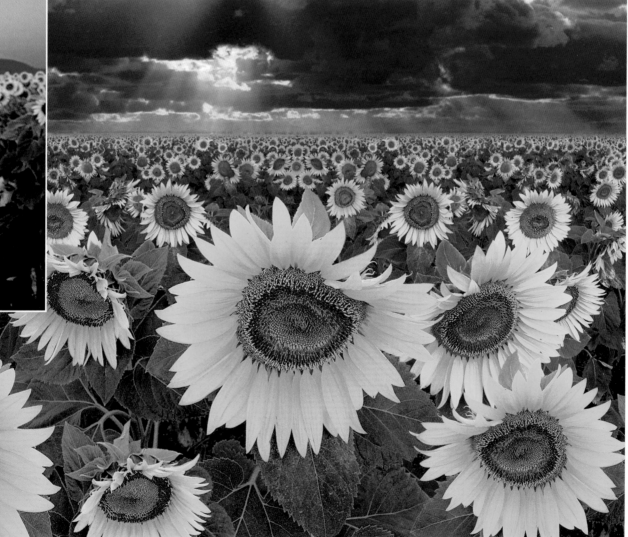

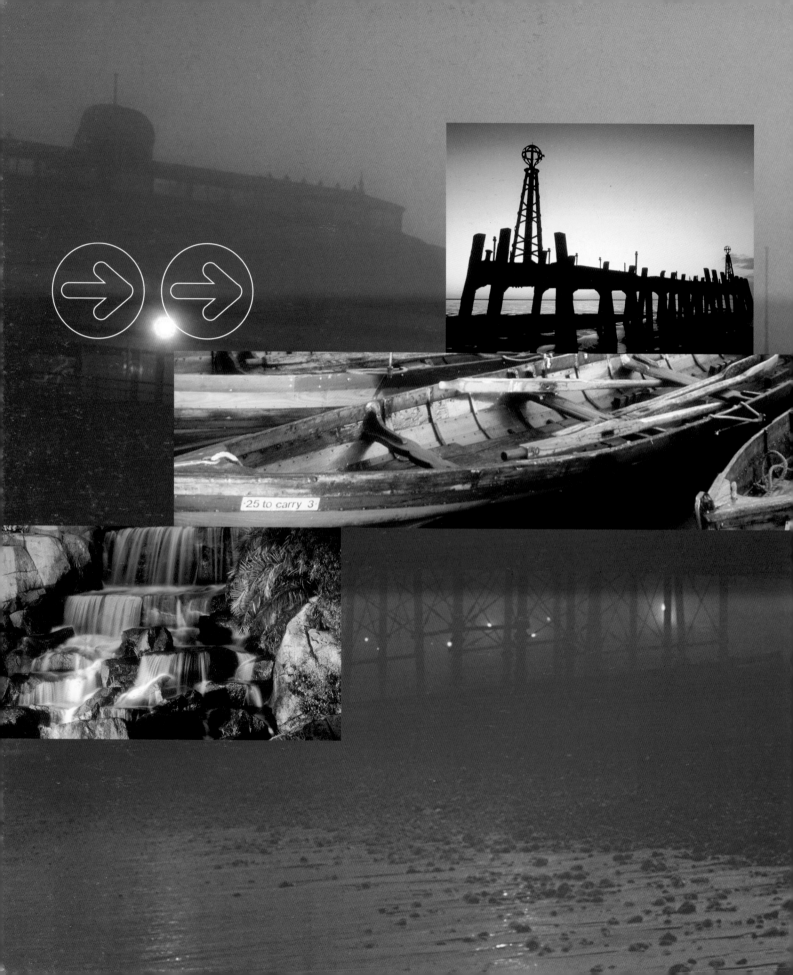

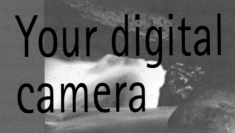

1 Your digital camera

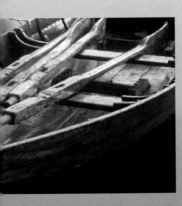

Once the poor relative of the film camera, the digital camera is rapidly approaching a point where it will match and even better its precursor. In fact, if the new technology has a weakness, it's the frantic rate of obsolescence. Whatever camera you buy, it will only be a few months before a better model appears. This makes it crucial to know what you are buying before you splash out. Take a deep breath and get ready to jump into the digital world.

The camera and its controls

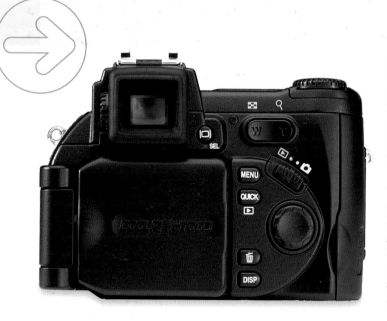

The rear of the Nikon Coolpix 5700, an excellent mid-range digital camera. Visible on the left are the viewfinder and, below, the swiveling LCD monitor. On the right you can see the buttons and control pad for navigating the menus, the flap covering the card slots, and the zoom control.

Before making the leap into the digital age, it is essential to have an understanding of the various components that make up a digital camera. This simple guide illustrates the differences between traditional and digital cameras.

CCD (CHARGE-COUPLED DEVICE)

These are usually two-thirds of an inch in size and are used in place of film to capture the image as it exposes. Each CCD is made up of tiny light-sensitive silicon photo diodes that capture the light as it shines on them.

LENS/DIGITAL ZOOM

Ignore the digital zoom ratio and look out for the optical resolution. The greater the optical zoom range, the better. Digital cameras do suffer from not having very wide-angle focal lengths. The widest is usually 7.0 to 8.0mm, which ranks as the equivalent of a 35mm wide-angle lens.

AUTO-FOCUS/AUTO-FOCUS MODES

Most cameras offer manual or auto-focus modes. More sophisticated models have five-area multi auto-focus. You can choose which area in the frame your subject will be in and the auto-focus will concentrate in that area.

From above the camera you can see the shutter release and the mode dial on top of the handgrip, the LCD panel, which displays useful information on exposure and shots remaining, and the accessory shoe, which allows connection to an external flash unit.

LCD MONITOR/VIEWFINDER

One of the most obvious benefits of shooting digitally is that you can see what you've just shot on a color screen. Try to get a camera that also has a standard optical viewfinder.

STORAGE

Most cameras use Compact Flash or Smart Media cards, but you can also find Memory Stick, SD Memory Card, XD Memory Card, and Microdrive. The last format offers the highest storage capacity of up to 4 Gigabytes. Other cards come in sizes from 16 to 512 Megabytes.

CAPTURE MODES

Most cameras have the option to shoot in several file formats. In most cases, the best is TIFF. Some higher-spec cameras offer a RAW file format, smaller in size than a Tiff but still retaining all the original data. The last option is usually a compressed JPEG format. JPEGs are smaller, so you can pack more onto a memory card, but there is always some loss in quality. Having said that, the highest quality setting still provides good results.

SHUTTER

While not all digital cameras have shutters, most have a control that simulates the effects of shutter speed in film photography. If you are interested in night shots and low-light photography, then make sure that the camera is able to take long exposures. A shutter speed of 15-30 seconds is essential. Expensive cameras can shoot several frames per second, but for most landscape work that's irrelevant.

APERTURE

The aperture, also known as an iris or diaphragm, is a hole at the end of the lens that has up to seven blades to create the round shape needed. This and the shutter speed control the exposure and depth of field.

EXPOSURE CONTROL

More sophisticated cameras have several modes to choose from, including auto, program, aperture priority, shutter priority, scenes, and manual. Scene mode usually has several settings, such as landscape, portrait, night, and so on, are good starting points for a beginner.

EXPOSURE METERING

More sophisticated cameras offer a wider choice of modes to choose from. These include segment or matrix metering on most models.

EXPOSURE RANGE

The exposure value or EV range can be from -2.0 to +18.0, which would equate to using ISO 100, 200, 400 and 800 speed film. The ISO rating is an internationally recognized standard for the light sensitivity of film. The higher the ISO, the more sensitive the CCD.

SENSITIVITY

The sensitivity of a CCD is referred to as its dynamic range. The higher the figure, the better. Background noise has always been a problem with digital cameras, especially in low-light situations. When the CCD can't pick up enough information, it creates patterns of white pixels which show up in dark areas.

WHITE BALANCE

White balance is used to correct any color casts present in the shot. Most cameras allow an auto white balance to be taken, and some cameras allow the white balance to be changed using preset modes.

FLASH

Most digital cameras come with a small built-in flash. For more serious work you need to buy a separate hand-held flashgun.

BATTERY

Digital cameras are battery-hungry. When using the LCD monitor and downloading to a storage card, you use a lot of power. Rechargeable batteries offer the best route to economy.

IMAGE RESOLUTION/FILE SIZE

The image size and resolution of a picture directly relate to the size of the file you save to your memory card or the hard disk. Digital cameras come in a variety of resolutions : usually known as megapixel ratings. More expensive cameras have higher megapixel ratings: top-of-the-range models are now capable of capturing up to 15 million pixels, but the quality of even 3-megapixel cameras can be surprisingly good.

▶ A 3-megapixel camera uses a maximum pixel size of 2100 x 1500. At 72ppi it can produce a 29 x 21-inch print, but at the recommended printer resolution of 300ppi it will only produce a file size of 7 x 5 inches.

▶ A 5-megapixel camera can produce a print of 8.5 x 6.4 inches at 300ppi.

▶ A 6-megapixel camera can produce a print of 14 x 9.5 inches at 300ppi.

The front of the Nikon Coolpix 5700, showing the shutter release, the 8x optical zoom lens, and the flash. The Coolpix 5700 uses a 5-megapixel CCD—to get better image quality you would need to go higher up the price range to a digital SLR camera.

TIP Buy a camera with a good zoom range or an SLR with interchangeable lenses for maximum flexibility. Get the best you can afford. Skimping only leaves you disappointed and desperate to upgrade.

The lens

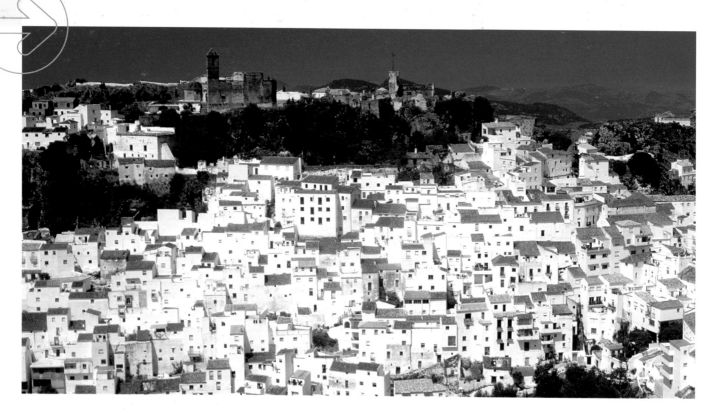

Choosing a lens suitable for the shots you plan to take is of paramount importance. The wide diversity of lenses available to photographers can be mind-boggling. Although some lenses have distinct advantages over others in certain situations, you will find that your digital camera's built-in lens is more than capable.

Lenses have two main controls—the aperture and the focus. The aperture is a diaphragm that opens and closes, allowing more or less light in. In conjunction with the shutter speed, this controls the exposure. The lens also rotates to focus from close-up to infinity.

Having the right lens for the right job is essential. Most digital cameras come with a fixed zoom lens, which will suffice. Choose a camera that has a good range from wide-angle to telephoto. Most fall down at the wide end of the zoom. If you are making the change from conventional-film SLR cameras, you will find many digital cameras can't manage much more than 35mm or 28mm at most.

Most digital camera use a CCD sensor size smaller than the traditional 35mm camera film size, which effectively makes lenses about 1.5 times longer. A 28mm lens thus becomes a 42mm lens on a digital camera.

If you like your shots super-wide or super-long, you may need to buy a pro SLR digital camera with interchangeable lenses. If you already own such exotic lenses, this could be your best route. The latest 13-megapixel cameras have full-frame 35mm size CCDs.

WIDE-ANGLE LENSES 20MM–45MM

Even at 28mm such a lens would only just be considered wide-angle these days—14–20mm is now the norm. With digital photography, however, it is possible to use a shorter focal length with success. Indeed, "panoramic stitchers" exist that allow panoramic shots to be made by joining together several shots.

The other strength of wide-angles is depth of field (see page 17). Most shots will have foreground to background sharpness at f8 or more. Only when shooting a subject at closer range will smaller apertures be needed to maintain front-to-back sharpness.

Wide-angle lenses have a dynamic effect on landscapes. Sweeping vistas take on a feeling of fantastic depth because more can be taken in than the angle of natural vision.

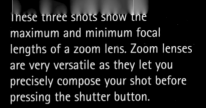

The lens

These shots illustrate how zooming in on a subject can isolate detail within the wider shot. How far you can zoom in depends on your lens' focal range. Wide-angle and telephoto converters can be fitted to a lens to give it extra range. Try to buy a camera with the widest optical zoom range that you can afford.

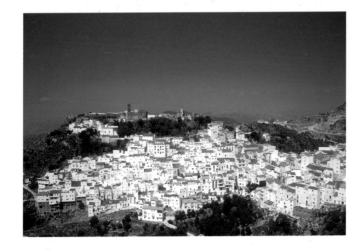

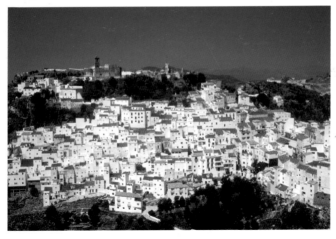

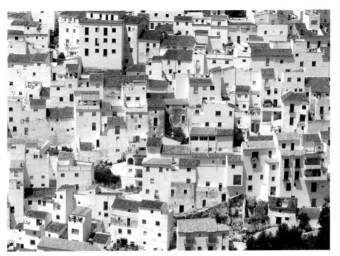

STANDARD LENSES TO SHORT TELEPHOTO 50MM–135MM

A 45–50mm focal length is similar in angle of view to our own field of vision. It brings things a little closer, but without the severity of a telephoto. It is good practice to slow down the zooming process and look at the world at several stops on the way.

The short telephoto of 90–135mm is known as the ideal portrait lens. It brings the subject in fairly close, but gives a little breathing space between you and them. Telephoto compression starts to take effect where distant objects begin to appear layered one on top of another. Depth of field becomes shallower and throws the background nicely out of focus on close subjects, such as people or flowers. This helps to isolate the subject and throw more importance on them. This focal length is good for removing ugly problems, such as garbage or parking lots in the foreground.

TELEPHOTO LENSES 150MM–400MM AND BEYOND

Telephoto compression and magnification really become apparent at these focal lengths. Buildings and mountains start to fall over one another to get to your lens!

Depth of field becomes almost non-existent, the longer the lens and greater the magnification, but this lets a subject be sharply outlined against a very blurred background. A tripod should be used to allow for smaller apertures—this will give greater depth of field when required.

Digital SLR cameras with interchangeable lenses allow the use of ultra-long and fast telephoto lenses up to 1000mm. These are aimed mainly at professional wildlife and sports photographers, but offer staggering magnification of the subject. Camera shake is magnified proportionately so a very steady hand or a tripod is essential. Canon, Nikon, and Sigma all produce Image Stabilizer lenses that use gyroscopic motors to reduce camera shake—yes, they do work!

Focusing

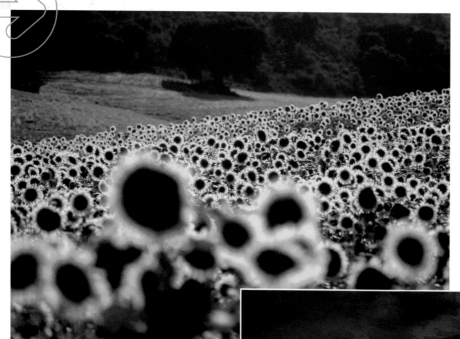

 This is a perfect example of differential focusing. The foreground has been allowed to go out of focus on purpose in order to create an artistic effect. This is easier to achieve with a lens that is set to telephoto, as in this case, because the depth of field is less anyway.

TIP → Learn to use manual focusing as it is always more reliable and precise in the long run, especially when you are taking photographs in low light.

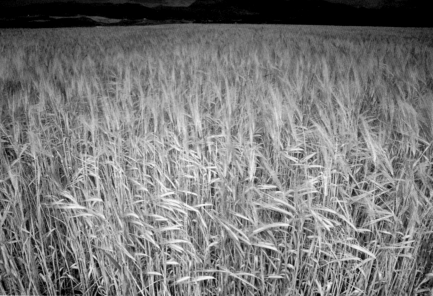

Whether with fixed zoom or interchangeable lenses, digital cameras use auto-focus to control the focusing. On some models this can be switched to manual for tricky situations or when you want to override the camera. On the whole, technology has made auto-focus fast and reliable. Fast-moving action such as motor racing benefits hugely from it, but very few landscapes need fast auto-focus! Indeed, auto-focus is usually biased to the center of the frame, and that is no good for many situations. Some cameras let you alter the bias from one area of the frame to the next, but manual focusing is often best for precise control.

Keep an eye out for times when your auto-focus system fails to work properly. In this case the wheat was very dark (it had to be lit with fill-in flash) and the lens struggled to find something to lock onto when focusing. Either focus and use the focus lock button or set the camera to focus manually, as I did here. Very dark or light scenes with little contrast between foreground and background are always going to fool the auto-focus, so learn how to focus manually. My camera is on manual focus all the time, unless I am shooting a fast-moving subject. You'll find that most mountains and cities stay quite still!

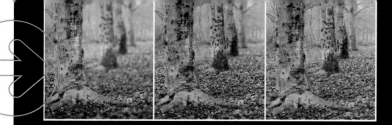

These shots show how the lens aperture affects the depth of field in a photograph. By gradually stopping down the aperture from f2 to f8 to f16 you can see that the zone of sharpness extends dramatically. This effect is a very powerful tool that can be used with great success.

Hyper-focal focusing is a technique that relies on using the depth-of-field scale for maximum sharpness. If you have such a scale on your lens, move the infinity focus symbol on the right of the scale to where it displays your chosen aperture setting. This allows nearer objects to remain sharp. Depth of field covers two-thirds in front of your point of focus and one-third behind.

In practice, you can manually focus one-third of the way in, which usually gives adequate depth of field when used with a small aperture and wide-angle setting. If your camera does not have manual focus, it should have a focus lock button. This freezes the focus when pressed to let you recompose your shot.

Depth of field at longer focal lengths will be determined by the effect you desire. Choose a large aperture to create minimal depth of field. Long lenses and small apertures means you need a tripod for maximum sharpness, or camera shake will ruin the shot.

UNDERSTANDING DEPTH OF FIELD

Depth of field is the zone of sharpness in a photograph: the area before and after the point of focus at where the scene remains in sharp focus. Depth of field is controlled by your aperture setting, the focal length of the lens and the point of focus. The aperture is a diaphragm that controls the amount of light entering a lens and falling onto the CCD sensor. A large aperture of f2 will let in more light than a small aperture of f8. It also gives a smaller depth of field than a smaller aperture. The shorter the focal length, the greater the depth of field is. The longer the lens gets, the shallower the depth of field.

Any lens will have its maximum depth of field at infinity. The closer you get to a subject, the more this reduces the depth of field. For the greatest depth of field use a wide-angle lens with a small aperture, and for minimal depth of field use a long telephoto lens with a wide aperture.

DIFFERENTIAL FOCUS

This technique is the opposite to hyper-focal focusing. Here the object is to create a deliberately narrow depth of field. This is done to put emphasis on the subject and throw the background totally out of focus. It is also a creative technique used for photographing relatively close-up objects such as flowers. Here close focusing makes the subjects deliberately large in the frame, and by using the widest aperture only a tiny part remains in detail. This is a very effective and artistic technique that works well on detail shots.

The longer the focal length is, the closer the focus; the wider the aperture, the more pronounced the effect becomes. Choose a small object to photograph, zoom in with the lens, and use the widest aperture available to your lens. A tripod is often essential to allow precise focusing on one part of the subject. Try several shots, each with a smaller aperture, and choose the one that pleases you the most.

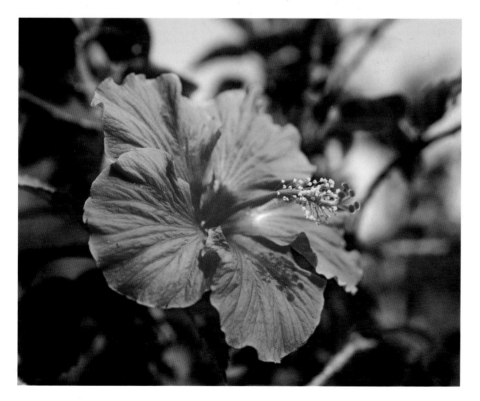

Shooting close up to a subject will also allow differential focus to be used. Flowers are great for isolating tiny detail and letting the rest of the image go out of focus. Even when using small apertures, close-up (or macro) photography automatically reduces the depth of field, and depth of field diminishes the closer you get. You can sometimes end up with only a few millimeters in focus.

Exposure

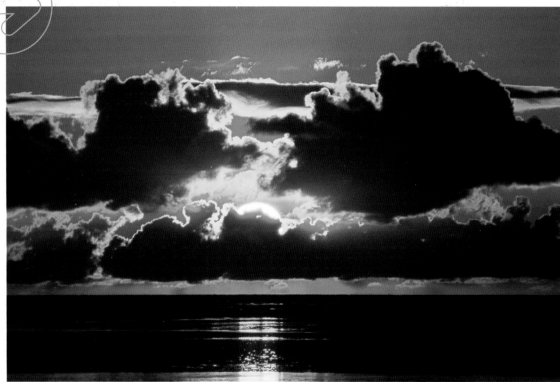

You can't beat a good sunset. It's nature's dramatic end to the day. All the right ingredients were in place for a stunner—great clouds to add a sense of drama, water for reflections, and the sun poking through the clouds just enough so that flare wasn't a problem.

Achieving the correct exposure for a shot is far from being an exact science. Often, it is far more useful to shoot a range of images at different exposures and then choose the best image at the editing stage. Here we highlight the different exposure techniques that are available to the photographer.

A fairly average shot that should cope well with any exposure mode. This is perfectly suited to matrix or center-weighted metering. Here a polarizing filter was used to add extra impact to the sky.

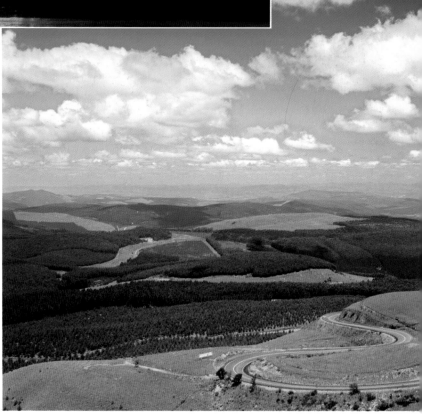

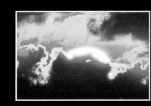
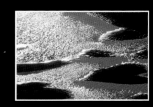

Automatic exposure is perfectly acceptable for general shots, but understanding how exposures work and manually adapting the exposure will let you go that extra hurdle and create really stunning shots.

SPOT METERING

Here the camera uses a very narrow spot in the center of the frame to analyze the light levels. This is a very accurate method of metering if you know where to point. Try taking a highlight and shadow reading and average them out. More sophisticated cameras will do the math for you! You can also take a reading from a mid-tone area of the scene.

CENTER-WEIGHTED METERING

A less sophisticated metering system that still works well for normal scenes. The whole scene is measured, with preference being given to the center where the subject normally is. Point the camera away from extreme bright or dark areas and take an average of the scene.

MULTIPLE ZONE METERING

Multiple zone metering is the state-of-the-art metering system. The frame is divided into different zones (up to 256 in top digital cameras) and the light is measured from each zone with a bias to the center of the shot.

GRAY CARD

In-camera or hand-held reflected light exposure meters are calibrated to a standard 18% mid-tone gray reflectance from the subject. In theory, this will give a perfect exposure. This is fine if your subject is 18% gray, but most are not. You have to learn how to tweak the exposure reading of your camera in order to create a correct exposure.

A rough guide is to overexpose bright scenes by 1 to 1½ stops and bracket around this reading. The opposite is true when metering from dark subjects—in this situation underexpose by 1 to 1½ stops from the camera reading. Green grass, trees, and mid-tone rocks/earth are all good for getting an average 18% gray reading.

TIP Learning to expose manually is a great advantage. Ultimately, this will enhance your ability to create the right mood for your shots, particularly in low-light conditions.

The contrast range in a shot doesn't get much higher than this: pure blacks next to pure whites. Here the camera tries to lighten the shot, turning it to 18% gray and ruining the lovely dark moody quality to the image. There are three options open to you for metering. First, take a reading from the dark area and decrease exposure by 1 to 1½ stops; second, take a reading from the highlights and increase exposure by the same amount; and third, take a reading from both areas and divide the two to get the right setting. 1/125 at f8 for the highlight, for example, and 1/60 at f8 for the shadows.

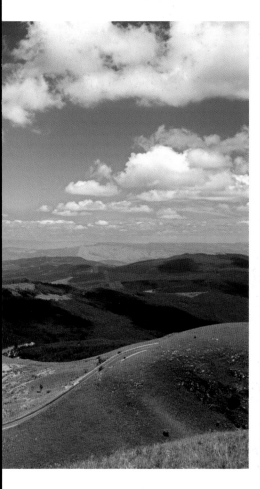
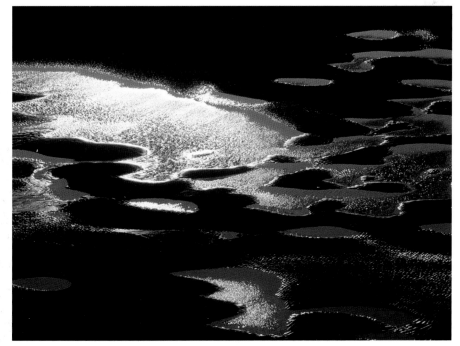

Exposure

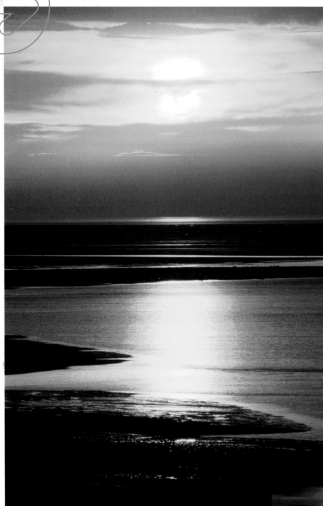

WHITE BALANCE

Tungsten lighting has a yellow color cast. If you stand outside a house or store, you can see the yellow color of the shop lights. Go inside and your brain will correct this effect.

The human brain can quickly adapt to various light sources and adjust them automatically to a more natural daylight effect. In essence, this is the same technique that digital cameras use to correct color casts from artificial and natural light sources. Digital cameras use the white balance to correct any color casts. It can be adjusted manually or automatically. The white balance becomes more critical under artificial lighting situations. The camera will adjust the light to be bluer under artificial lights. If you have daylight coming in through windows, you will notice it goes very blue. This is similar to the old-fashioned technique of putting a blue filter over your lens.

As an experiment, try shooting a white sheet of paper in manual mode using the lighting conditions that you will be shooting under. This should give a fairly accurate color correction. Some newer models will even bracket the white balance, giving a neutral, blue and red variation of the color.

The three shots on this page illustrate bracketing. The correct exposure (shown here) was achieved by taking a meter reading to the side of the sun, keeping it out of the frame. I recomposed the shot afterward.

Left to its own devices the camera meter will underexpose the shot and make it too dark (left). With overexposure there is more detail visible in the shore, but the light areas in the sky and on the relective surface of the sea blow out (right).

BRACKETING

Most digital cameras will let you bracket your shots by producing an underexposed, correct, and overexposed version with one click of the button. You can then preview the variations and delete ones that don't work.

TIP With scenes that have areas of very strong contrast you can bracket several shots and use software to create a digital composite from the best bits of each, so creating the effect of one perfect exposure.

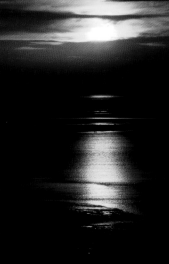

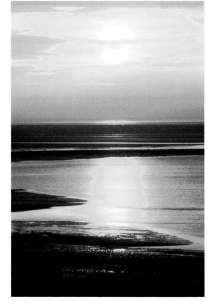

A classic shot that is often ruined by poor exposure. The highly reflective white snow causes underexposure, turning the snow gray. Simply remember to increase exposure by 1½ to 2 stops. You can dial this in using the exposure compensation dial on your camera.

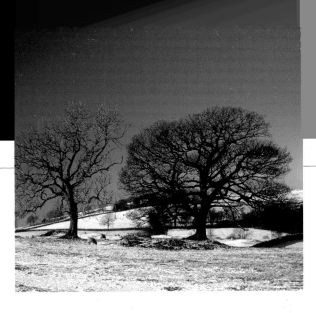

FACT FILE

f-stops/apertures

The aperture in a lens through which light travels to the CCD plane is called the iris/diaphragm. It has been designed to open and close in incremental steps called f-stops. Most interchangeable lenses have full and half f-stop increments, while most fixed zoom cameras will use 1/3 incremental steps for finer control. Expensive lenses usually have a larger aperture and therefore make faster shutter speeds possible. A lens with a maximum aperture of f2 will, for example, allow two stops' more light than a lens of f4. This is very useful in low light conditions.

APERTURE

Maximum									Minimum	
f1.2	f1.4	f1.8	f2	f2.8	f4	f5.6	f8	f11	f16	f22
1/2000	1/1000	1/500	1/250	1/125	1/60	1/30	1/15	1/8	1/4	1/2

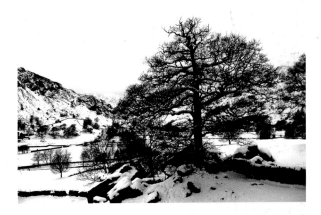

Shutter speeds (above in seconds)

Once the correct combination of aperture and shutter speed have been chosen for the exposure, the following rule applies:

▶ One f-stop increase (from f4 to f2.8) admits double the light of the previous one, so the shutter speed has to be halved to compensate (i.e., 1/125 at f2.8).

▶ One f-stop decrease (from f4 to f5.6) admits half the light of the previous one, so the shutter speed has to be doubled to compensate (i.e., 1/30 at f5.6).

Automated exposure programs

These are built in programs that allow automated exposure, depending on which subject you are shooting.

Auto program (P)

The camera will choose the correct aperture/shutter speed for the exposure and will use stored exposure situations to come up with the best combination. You can usually change the aperture or shutter speed to suit your own requirements.

Shutter priority (S)

Enables you to set your desired shutter speed and the camera automatically selects the aperture for correct exposure. Shutter priority can be used to freeze fast-moving action or slow down the speed for blurred motion effects.

Aperture priority (A)

Enables you to set your desired aperture and the camera controls the best shutter speed for correct exposure. Aperture priority can be used to control depth of field. A large aperture will give shallow depth of field, while a small aperture will allow depth of field to be maximized for any given point of focus.

Low light

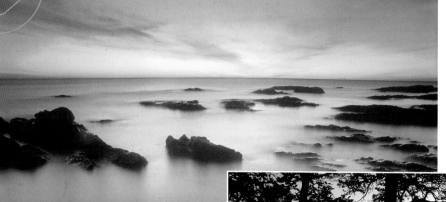

This seascape was shot at sunrise, where pre-dawn light is soft and full of color. The challenge is working quickly, as the shift to daylight will spoil the effect.

This seascape was shot at sunrise, where pre-dawn light is soft and full of color. The challenge is working quickly, as the shift to daylight will spoil the effect.

This forest was shot at dusk, when the light takes on more color. You can shoot until dark with a shutter speed of over 30 seconds, yielding interesting color shifts as well.

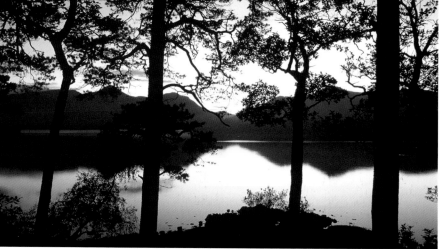

Low-light photography is a technical challenge that seems quite daunting, but with experience will become a very important part of your repertoire. Generally, low-light levels occur after the sun has gone down but there are many days when the general light levels are low, especially during the winter.

The first challenge may be to get an exposure reading in the first place. If you are having trouble, open up the lens to maximum aperture and then take a reading. For every f-stop you close down, you must double the exposure. If you close down, 3 stops from a reading of, say, 5 seconds at f2.8, your new reading will be 10 seconds at f4 and finally 20 seconds at f5.6.

Nighttime shots are the most difficult to pull off, with noise levels a major problem. This is a grainy effect noticeable in shadows and is caused by a lack of sensitivity in the CCD to pick up and record information in dark shadow areas. Newer cameras use various techniques, such as double exposures and a built-in noise reduction mode, to compensate for this; they also have more sensitive CCDs with a higher dynamic range. Landscapes need light in order to see them—but how much light? The afterglow of a sunset can last for 30 minutes or so and leave enough light to record if you adopt long exposures. How long an exposure will depend on the subject and its reflectance values. Photographing deep within a forest can leave you struggling with long exposures even during the day. Most landscape subjects will have limited time before the exposure times become unmanageable.

CALCULATING EXPOSURE TIMES

Exposing for low-light does not need to be scary. Use the averaged camera exposure as a starting point. Also, bracket your exposures, as camera meters can often be fooled into underexposure. Usually you will only need to bracket to longer exposures, as underexposure is rarely a problem in these conditions.

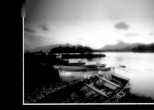 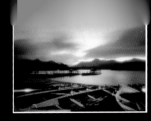

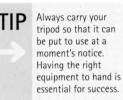

Taking photographs in low light levels unfailingly creates mood and impact. Find the right subject matter and you can't fail to take stunning shots. In these pictures, I used car headlights for an unusual effect.

The impact of this beautiful mosque in Marbella, Spain was enhanced by shooting it at dusk, when it was also lit up by electric lighting to add to the drama. I made sure that the sky still retained some color for added contrast, to bring out the detail of the silhouetted palm trees and the tall, narrow poplars in the background.

TIP → Always carry your tripod so that it can be put to use at a moment's notice. Having the right equipment to hand is essential for success.

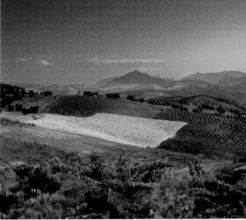

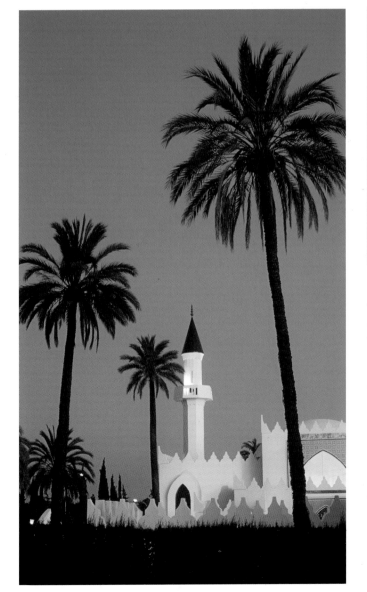

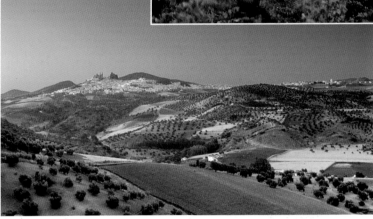

ISO SETTINGS

The ISO setting on your camera lets you change the sensitivity of the CCD so that you can use faster shutter speeds at low light levels.

Unlike conventional film, where you had to change the entire film to alter the ISO sensitivity, you can change the ISO setting on a per shot basis with digital cameras. The snag is a loss of quality, the higher the ISO setting you use. Extra noise and some color shifts are possible side effects. If you then use a compressed file format other than RAW/TIFF, you will add to these quality problems. These are correctable, but for top quality use the finest ISO setting (usually ISO 100) and steady the camera for long exposures (digital photography still entails lugging a tripod around, I'm afraid!).

The top picture was shot 15 minutes after sunset, with a polarizer used to boost color saturation in both sky and land. The lower shot, of the "white village" of Olvera, Spain, was taken as the last rays of the sun hit the town. The colors are created by the natural beauty of the evening sunlight.

Using flash

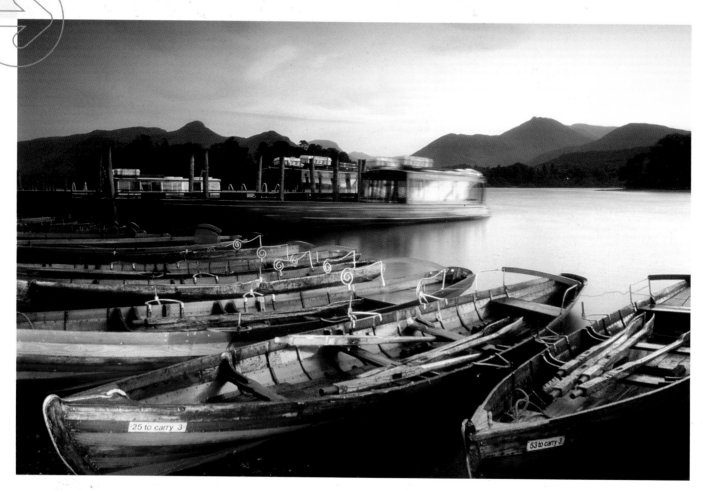

Flash is rarely used in most landscape shots, but there are instances when a burst of fill-in flash can help to liven up a scene. There are two main options open to you for flash photography: using a built-in camera flash or appending additional external flashguns.

Built-in flashguns can fill-in a dark foreground subject and make it brighter if it is close enough, but they do have limitations because they are not overly powerful. Their main use will be to illuminate a subject such as flowers, which are close enough to the camera to be affected by the flash. Most flashguns have a range of approximately 0.5m to 4.0m (1.7 ft to 13 ft), which means that distant landscapes cannot be lit by the camera's built-in flash. Modern built-in flashguns will usually calculate the exposure for you. If you buy an additional flashgun for your camera (which can often be linked by an extension cord for greater freedom), stick to the same manufacturer, as most cameras will be able to communicate with these to maintain accurate flash exposures.

It is possible to produce some exciting shots if you have access to a more powerful hand-held flashgun that can be moved around independently of the camera. This can be used for a technique called "painting with light."

This is best suited to low-light photography so you have ample time to build up the flash with multiple exposures. Set the camera up on a tripod and set to either your longest exposure or multiple exposure, if your camera has this function. A multiple exposure facility will make this technique much easier as it lets you re-expose the same frame again and again and build up a much greater flash effect.

With the camera shutter fired, you can then operate the flash as many times as you want within the length of exposure chosen. Some

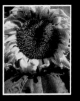

The use of fill-in flash can add graphic impact to a shot and will reduce unwanted shadows. Objects that are close to the camera will need smaller apertures than wide angle shots, which will need wide apertures.

Here my car headlights were shone onto the boats, for added detail in the shadows. This kind of improvised lighting can give extra dimension and lift to a shot.

Notice how the fill-in flash falls away in the background due to insufficient flash power, though it has actually created an interesting effect in this case.

cameras will expose for several minutes, which is plenty of time to fire off numerous flashes. It is best to run about the scene and fire from different locations. Don't put yourself between the flash and the camera or it will record your silhouette. Try hiding behind objects in order to avoid this.

For every f-stop you close down your lens, the flash output has to be doubled to maintain the same exposure. For this reason it is best to use a wide aperture. Only experimentation with your own flash set-up will tell you the optimum aperture. Once this has been found, you can keep using the same aperture again and again.

Using several flashguns simultaneously is going to give greater flexibility and allow the flash exposure to be built up a lot more

quickly. Most flashguns can be fired remotely by attaching a slave unit via a cord. Place this slave so that it can see your main flash, and when you fire your main flashgun, it will automatically fire the remote flashgun. Flashguns are expensive, so look out for some second-hand ones.

"IMPROVISING" FLASH

Alternative light sources are car headlights. I have successfully placed my car so that the beam illuminates the subject. Car headlights offer a very powerful light source to experiment with. You can also try a powerful hand-held torch and paint with light: literally move the torch around during the long exposure so that the main subject is evenly illuminated all over.

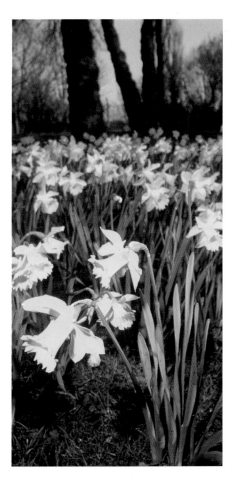

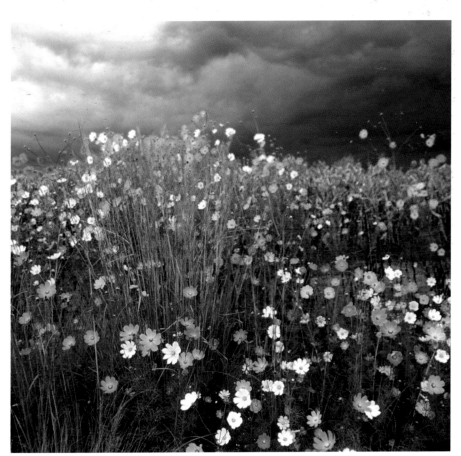

These cosmos flowers in South Africa were given a burst of fill-in flash from a Metz 45 - hand-held flash unit. This has helped to

brighten them against the stormy sky. I underexposed the shot by 1 stop, which has by default darkened the sky, adding to the effect.

Scanning

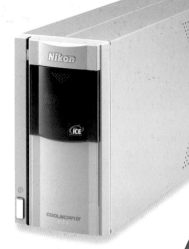

 Although this book is primarily aimed at people who have just bought a digital camera, you may, like me, have a closet full of old prints, film negatives, and transparencies. How do you deal with these? There are two basic methods of digitizing these—using a flatbed scanner or a dedicated film scanner.

Flatbed scanners are more versatile, and some include a built-in transparency hood. At 2400ppi you get excellent results.

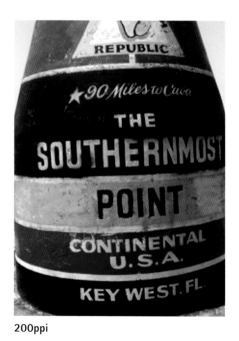

Film scanners are designed specifically to scan negatives, slides, and transparencies at very high resolutions.

FILM SCANNERS

Film scanners are not cheap, but have come down in price enormously in recent years. Most scanners are made for scanning 35mm film and will do a very good job. The top-of-

TIP Warped negatives/ transparencies can be placed in a slide mount to improve sharpness. Tape them down as well.

the-range scanners can scan at 4000dpi or more and usually come with some form of filter software that automatically removes scratches and dust.

Dynamic range is also an important consideration when purchasing a film scanner. Most cheap film scanners start at 3.0, but 3.4 to 3.8 is the norm for a decent scanner. Top-of-the-range film scanners go up to 4.0 and beyond and will capture very dense shadow detail and bright highlights. A transparency film has an average dynamic range from 3.0 up to

3.6. A scanner with a smaller dynamic range suffers from blown out highlights and very dark shadows often coupled with noise, as they cannot capture the wide contrast range. If using a cheaper film scanner, try to scan slightly overexposed shots for best results.

If you only need to scan a few shots, it may be more economical to use a system such as Kodak Photo CD. Here you send off your transparencies and Kodak will put them onto a CD that you can open up in an application such as Adobe Elements.

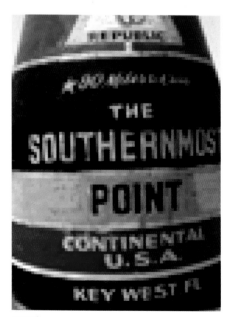

72ppi

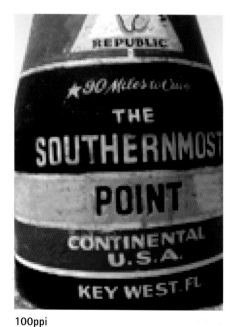

100ppi

200ppi

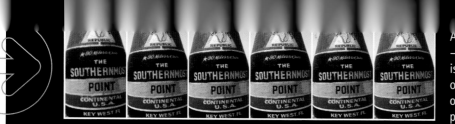

A good scanner is a wise investment, but —as with digital cameras—resolution is a key issue. The higher the resolution of your scanner, the higher the resolution of your image, and the larger it can be printed without any loss of detail.

FLATBED SCANNERS

If you have film negatives, you can use a film scanner or get them printed and use a flatbed scanner. Flatbed scanners are now very cheap and economical to buy, and even budget scanners offer good-quality scans. It is worth doing research first as this is such a vast market, but Epson, Microtek, and Agfa all do top-quality flatbed scanners. Some flatbed scanners even come with a transparency hood that lets you scan both slides and negatives. Try to get a flatbed with a dynamic range of 3.0 or more and a resolution of 2400ppi.

A flatbed scanner with a transparency hood that has a dynamic range of 3.6 or more is a serious piece of kit. It allows negative/transparency film and prints to be scanned to a high standard. It also lets you do experimental scanning with three-dimensional objects. Try scanning shells and using them in photomontages. Always use a protective glass/plastic sheet between the object and scanner.

RESOLUTION

Don't be deceived by flatbed scanners that seem to offer very high-interpolated resolutions. They are similar to digital cameras and the digital zoom/optical argument. Always go by the optical resolution. Higher resolutions are created by clever software, but it's not as clever as having the real power of optical resolution!

BIT DEPTH

The scanner's ability to record color and tonal detail. The greater the bit depth, the better the quality will be. Digital cameras work at 8 bits per channel (3 channels RGB = 24 bits in total), while some scanners work at 10, 12, or even 14 bits per channel. Software packages such as Adobe Elements convert all images to a default setting of 24 bits.

TIP Warm the flatbed scanner up for 20 minutes beforehand or you may get strange color casts appearing because the light source is still too cold. I normally let it do several pre-scans to warm it up.

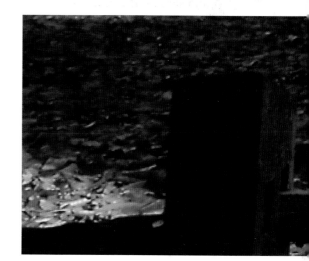

This example illustrates how problems can develop in a scan and in images captured by digital cameras. It is caused by lack of sensitivity in the dynamic range of the camera/scanner. This results in a build-up of unwanted artifacts called noise. It usually occurs in the darker areas where less sensitive CCDs struggle to pick up all the subtle shadow detail. It may also occur in the highlights, but the problem there is that the detail blows out to white.

This series of images demonstrates how increasing resolution improves the detail visible in a shot. Remember that resolution is the key to good-quality scans and prints. For Web use a resolution of 72–100ppi; for email use 100–300ppi (only use 300ppi if you have fast broadband access, or download times will be very long); for printing use 300–400ppi.

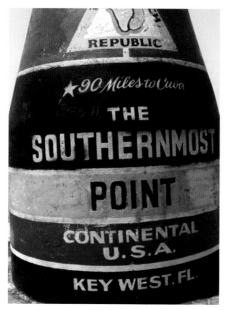

300ppi

400ppi

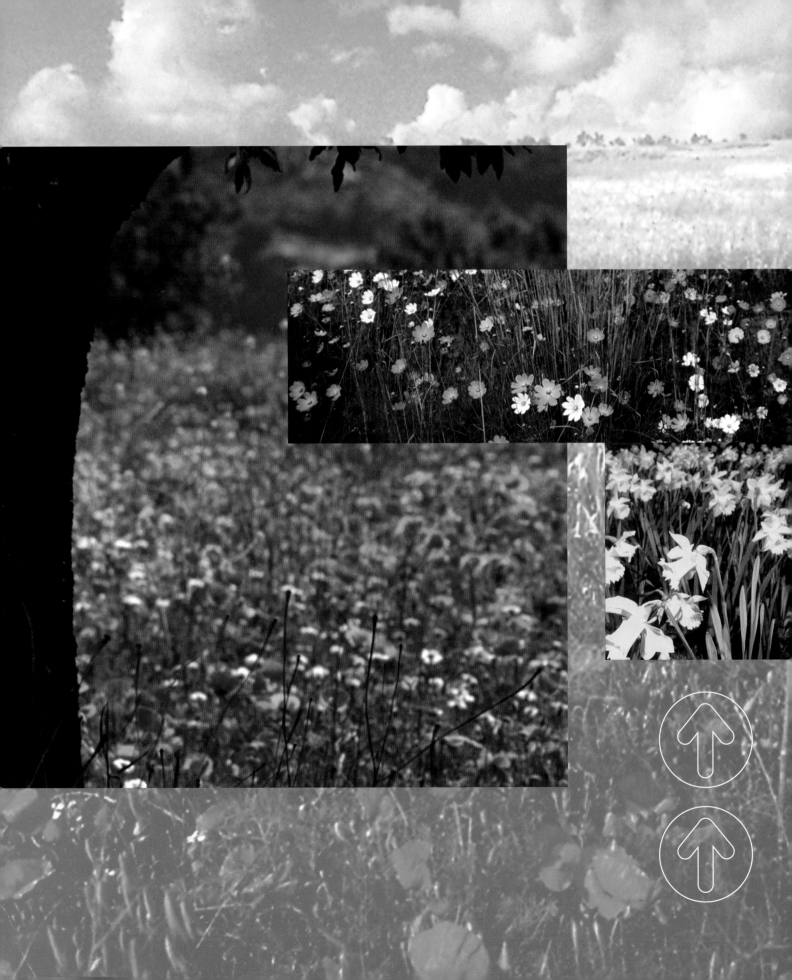

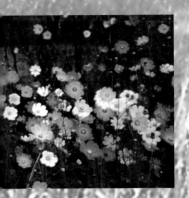

2 Taking great landscape shots

Landscapes have long been one of art's great themes, whether captured on canvas with paint or on film with a camera. Nature's beauty, color, and infinite variety will always amaze and inspire us. Film and high-street prints may have disappointed you in the past, seeming somehow to lose the magic of the moment, but with the control of digital photography you can capture—and even improve upon—what you see.

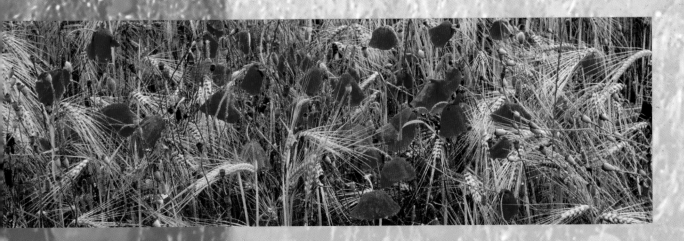

Capture the moment

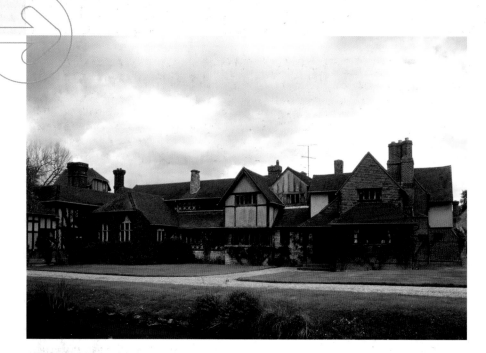

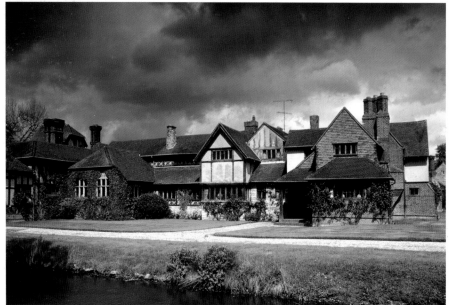

The difference that a few minutes can make! One minute I was despondent that the day was lost to gray, overcast weather conditions and the next the sun popped out, albeit for a few minutes. Just enough time to grab a shot. I used a gray grad filter over the lens to maintain detail in the now stormy sky.

TIP Some of the best landscape photographs are shot just after a storm has cleared. Dust settles, the air is fresh, and the sky can create some amazing colors.

Being in the right place at the right time is a skill that cannot be taught. To do this simply takes a great deal of time, patience, and perseverance—and not a little bit of good fortune as well. But don't be deterred: stick at it and the results will pay dividends.

Photography is about freezing a fleeting moment in time. Blink an eye or turn your head and it's gone for ever. I find it quite depressing that somewhere I'm missing a beautiful shot, but you can't be everywhere all the time. Which is why you must make the most of the time that you do have while you are out photographing.

Preparation and planning will take you a long way down the road to capturing a successful photograph. Reading books, postcards, and local literature will let you find the local beauty spots very quickly when traveling and give you plenty of time to concentrate on and assess good viewpoints for shots.

If the weather is not right, use the time to reconnoiter the area and work out what time of day will work best for the shot. A compass is an invaluable aid in determining where the sun sets or rises. Always remember that sunset times vary with the seasons and the longitude, so don't get caught out by arriving too late for the shot because your brain is still running on summer time.

Patience is the most important weapon in a photographer's arsenal. I've lost count of the number of missed shots that just didn't happen because of bad weather or because I got bored waiting. When you have waited for what seems like an eternity and the sun does pop out from behind a storm cloud, it is a revelation to the soul. This is one of the most uplifting experiences a photographer can have.

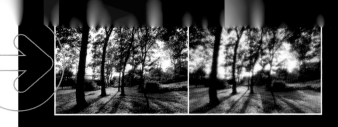

Low sun is great for strong backlit scenes such as this one in a local park, where raking shadows fall across the land. You can't always get away to exotic locations, and exploring your own back yard can yield shots that are just as satisfying, and you can shoot in interesting light more often as you can get on location quicker. Here I used a soft focus and warm-up filter to add impact.

Remember to dress for maximum comfort, depending on the season, for you will not feel inclined to wait if too wet or cold.

One ugly stormy day in Spain I was driving around a mountain road. It was gray and miserable, but as I rounded the bend, the sun popped out and I witnessed one of the most awesome sunsets of my life. The colors changed from pinks to orange to yellow. I was so engrossed with the shot that I forgot I was being soaked to the skin! Unpredictable weather is often the most exciting time to be shooting. It will usually be too horrible to shoot, but when the opportunity arises, you can't beat it.

All of this will let you be in the right place at the right time to click the shutter and walk off with a winner.

FACT FILE

Making life easier
If you can park your vehicle close enough to your viewpoint, you can set up your tripod and composition and then wait in the comfort of your car, while only your tripod gets wet and cold. You don't always need to suffer for your art!

When the sun pops out, remember that the aperture will need to be 1 or 2 stops smaller to stop overexposure if you are exposing manually.

Cover your camera with a clear plastic bag in the rain, held in place with rubber bands, or buy an all-weather protective housing. Always remember to wipe down your camera gear with a cloth if it gets wet.

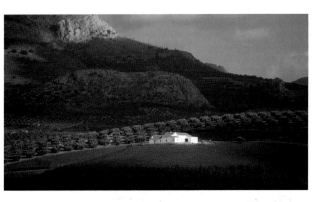

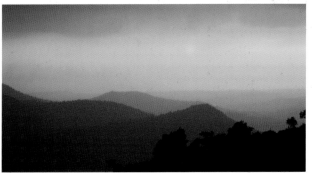

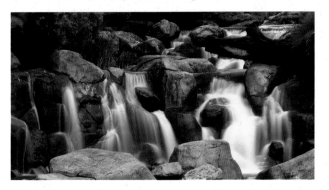

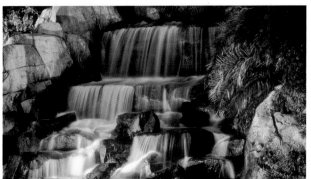

The sun lit up this Spanish finca or farmhouse as a break in the clouds appeared. This can be a frustrating time and patience is the key. You can often watch the sun as it moves closer, only to fizzle out at the last minute. I have waited for hours on occasion.

This is one of my most memorable sunsets shot in Spain. As I came around a corner in dismal rain, the clouds parted to reveal this amazing shot. It is natural, not filtered in any way, and the scene changed color several times.

These two shots show how the scene suddenly changes after the sun has disappeared. I like both shots, as they have very different yet equally valid moods. The blue shot, where the sun has disappeared is quieter and more reflective than the warmer, more vibrant sunny shot. Shoot under different lighting conditions to see the way color changes throughout the day and use this to your creative advantage.

Composition

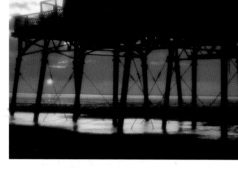

The pier was shot from below at low tide with a 35mm lens just as the sun was setting. I used a blur filter in Elements to soften the image for a moody effect.

This shot was taken with a telephoto lens. Note how the compression effect has filled the background with sand, and how the sun gives a beautiful backlit effect.

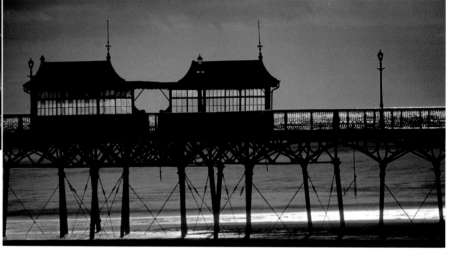

I n addition to a beautiful location bathed in gorgeous light, the next most important ingredient in a photograph is the photographer's ability to compose the shot properly. Poor composition will ruin even the best conditions that nature can place before us.

Knowing how and where to point your camera will increase your success rate dramatically. Because composition is a matter of personal taste, this is possibly the most difficult technique to master. All composition is based around there being a frame beyond which you cannot see. The secret to good composition is the art of filling this frame with a subject to create a harmonious group of elements that are pleasing to the eye. Fail to make a good composition and the eye is left to wander aimlessly around the picture, as it has no principal focal point. Clever composition can also help us to imagine what lies beyond the edge of the frame.

KEEP IT SIMPLE

The first basic rule is to keep it simple. Don't clutter the shot with too many elements until your confidence in composing grows. Less is definitely more! The secret is to remove any distracting elements from the frame. Indeed, placing only the subject in the frame is the best way to bring prominence to it. This may be a barn or farm on top of a hill, or a wall and gate in the foreground, or a combination of the two. Including other distracting elements at the side will weaken the shot considerably.

RULE OF THIRDS

There is a rule that aids in creating consistently good composition. Based on what the Greeks called the "Golden Section" and Leonardo called "Divine Proportion," it is entitled, the "rule of thirds" and was originally created to make classical Greek architecture look more

TIP It is advisable to wear rubber boots and use a tough camera bag when shooting in sandy, salty, or dusty conditions.

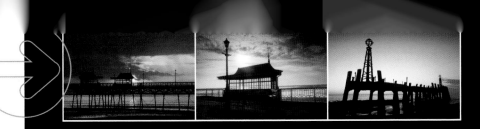

These three shots show how very different results can be achieved by arriving at different times of the day and viewing a location from different angles. Getting to know a subject by repeat visits is a good exercise.

beautiful. Basically, you need to mentally split the composition up into thirds horizontally and vertically. Placing your subject where any of the lines intersect will, in theory, produce a harmonious balance. But remember that rules are there to be broken as well! There are many variables, and as film isn't at a premium, there should be no excuses.

SHAPE AND FORM

All landscapes have shape and form, and your composition should help to bring out the best in them. Look out for strong shapes, such as circles, squares, rectangles, and triangles. Triangular or diagonal shapes are among the strongest and most dynamic shapes that you can find, particularly when used to split a shot into two or more zones of interest. Use shapes in a bold manner to add impact to your shots. Remember that color itself can create shapes, so use it to add power.

FOREGROUND/BACKGROUND INTEREST

It is important in most shots to have some form of foreground interest. The foreground may be the actual subject, with the rest of the shot being used as a background; or it may be used to draw the eye toward a subject farther back in the frame. It is important to balance the lighting and composition between the two areas. Foregrounds don't always have to have a prominent area of interest and importance. Open spaces such as deserts create their own context by having nothing in them. This very emptiness therefore becomes the subject. Usually, such shots rely on textures being lit by a sun low in the sky—light and form in harmony without distractions.

Foreground interest also brings out a feeling of depth. This is partly due to foreground perspective, whereby a nearer rock is clearly bigger than one of a similar nature farther

back in the scene. This is called diminishing scale perspective. Depth and scale within the picture are created by our own awareness of the relative size and shape that objects should be in the real world. Our brain is the storeroom for thousands of experiences; it uses these to work out what is going on in the shot. For example, an overhanging branch in the foreground with a small tree in the background gives a sense of depth. This is often called overlapping perspective.

Aerial perspective gives a feeling of depth by masking part of the landscape with fog, haze, or mist. Areas closest in will have little or no mist and appear strong and vibrant. Thus depth is created by dark tones in the foreground, with light tones receding into the distance.

The background (usually skies) should also not be overlooked. Ideally, a photograph should have a perfect balance between foreground and background.

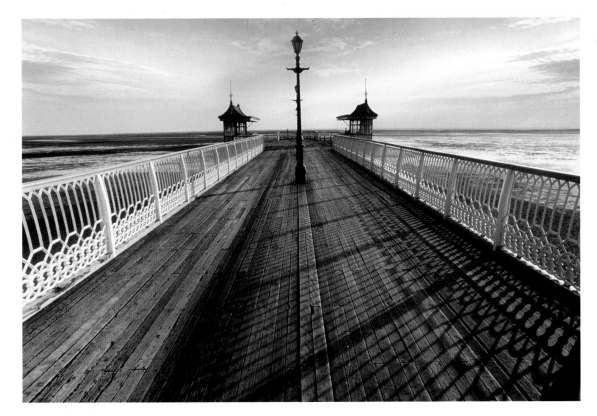

This late afternoon shot was made with a wide-angle lens and has caught the pier at its best with strong dynamic shadows bringing out texture in the wood and railings. If you look closely, you'll notice the sky was mirrored as it had blown out on the right-hand side. The lamp was placed in the center to create a sense of symmetry and the sky placed on the third.

Composition

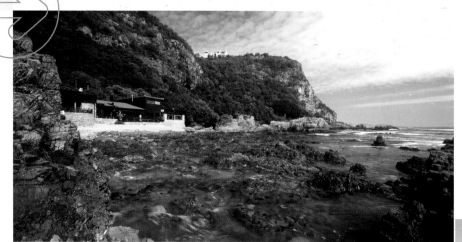

A low angle has accentuated the drama of these rocks and reduced the impact of the slightly cloudy sky.

By using a car and my feet, I managed to explore a large area of this lagoon and take photographs of it from several different angles during the course of one day.

LEAD-IN LINES

This is a handy trick, which uses the natural perspective of receding or converging lines to create foreground interest. Often, a strong triangular, three-dimensional shape is formed when two lead-in lines are used, such as in a bridge, path, river, fence, ploughed field, road, or wall. The long endless road running on for ever to the distant horizon is a classic example of the power of lead-in lines. The spot where the road eventually diminishes into nothing is known as the vanishing point.

LENS CHOICE

Depending on your lens choice, composition and focal point will change. Use a wide-angle lens for all-encompassing vistas. In general, the wider the lens, the greater the sense of depth and scale. If there are many layers in the frame, such as rolling hills, these will often give enough impact to carry the shot off on their own. Use the telephoto setting to isolate these parts of the landscape. It can also be used to remove unwanted foreground clutter, or to make your chosen subject matter more prominent within the shot.

PICTURE/IMAGE FORMAT

The most basic choice to make is: should you shoot horizontally (landscape) or vertically (portrait)? The most common format is landscape because the camera is designed with

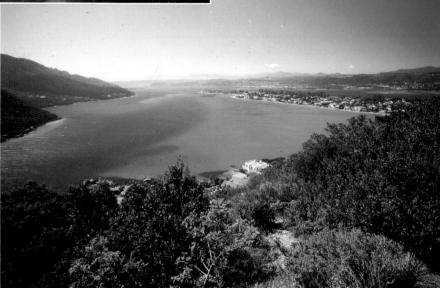

a horizontal viewing screen. Try using the portrait format for a whole day as an exercise to aid your compositional skills. Portrait shots suit tall, elongated subjects like trees.

It is possible on the computer to crop the basic frame top and bottom in order to create a wide but short panoramic format, or to zoom in tight to crop out unwanted detail. For maximum success, this will require top-quality files saved at the highest resolution that your camera is capable of. Cropping a small but highly compressed file will have disappointing end results, as the resolution will be too poor.

SYMMETRY

Symmetrical landscapes are not uncommon and provide an excellent opportunity to create new and interesting variations on the usual compositional rules. Look for lakes, rivers, sea, or any form of water or puddle. The main key to success is that the water must be perfectly still for maximum impact. Any wind blowing across the water and breaking it up into waves or ripples will ruin the shot. Sometimes very slightly off-centering the shot will lead to greater success. In this way, more emphasis may be given to the subject rather than to its reflection.

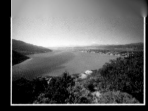
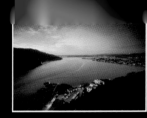

All the shots on these two pages were taken in one place—Knysna Lagoon, South Africa. Exploring the lagoon has yielded photographs showing many variations in the landscape of this one relatively small area.

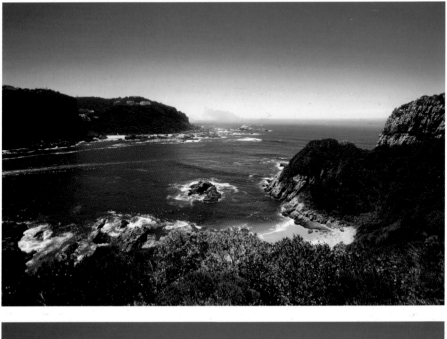

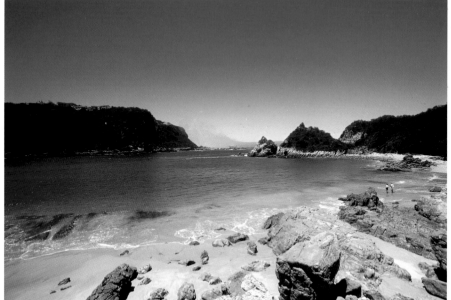

This side of the lagoon was a nature reserve and a boat was needed to gain access to it. The upper shot was taken from the top of the cliff, where the views were amazing. On the way back down to the boat I walked along the shore and used the rocks as foreground interest to lead the eye into the sweep of the lagoon (lower picture).

FACT FILE

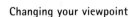

Changing your viewpoint

Changing your viewpoint can have a dramatic effect on your shot. Just by walking around your subject you can find many different angles to shoot from, all giving a new and interesting interpretation to the subject.

New photographers tend to remain static at their chosen location. They take a couple of shots near the parking lot. By stepping back from the shot and walking around, you can discover much more potential to your subject. Sometimes you may have to work very hard to get a good viewpoint. Be prepared to do some walking up steep hills!

Lowering the angle of viewpoint by tilting the camera or crouching down will give a dramatic increase to the feeling of apparent depth, especially with a wide-angle setting on your lens. This is a good way of avoiding having a boring sky in the frame. It also lets you concentrate on the foreground interest that is going to be your main subject matter. Good depth of field is essential in almost all cases, so use a tripod and watch out for any shadows that have been cast by you.

Getting up high is another means of changing your viewpoint. But looking down will not generally give you the same sense of foreground drama as choosing a viewpoint low to the ground. If you get up really high, this will allow sweeping panoramas to be taken. Often, though, simply standing on a brick wall can lift your shot above the ordinary.

Looking up at tall buildings can give an exaggerated sense of perspective known as converging verticals. Architectural purists may frown on this, but such a viewpoint often allows dynamic compositions to be created.

Framing

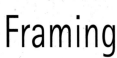

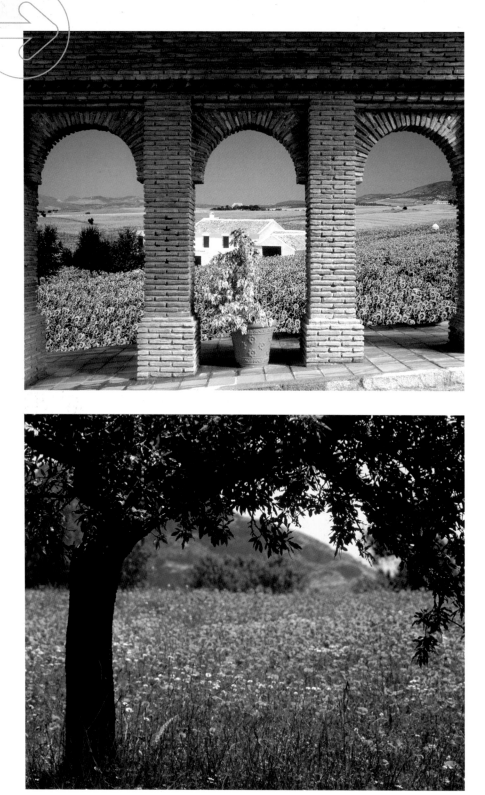

Choosing how to frame a scene can make or break a photograph. A good sense of composition is absolutely essential. Fortunately, digital photography lets photographers recompose their pictures at their leisure on the computer desktop. This can enable you to transform a good photograph into a great one, given the right subject matter.

A good compositional trick is to look for something to frame your subject, such as a tree or archway. This is a great way of placing emphasis on your subject. Framing a subject can give it an air of mystery, as though you are peering into a place from a hiding position. It can also help to cement the subject within the landscape and give a shot more impact. Always keep an eye out for different ways to interpret your subject. Spend time looking and walking around your subject to find the different possibilities that unfurl as you view it from different perspectives.

Using a natural frame can help to hide any ugly and distracting areas that would otherwise ruin the shot. A car or a boring sky can be effectively removed from the composition without weakening it. If no natural frame is available, it is still possible to add a frame later on in Adobe Photoshop

The original shot was a good mixture of texture and light. I removed the inside of the arches, then put the farm on a new layer behind the archway.

The tree was used to create a frame around the poppies in the background. I used a telephoto setting and tripod for sharpness.

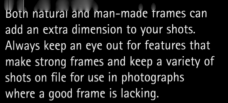

Both natural and man-made frames can add an extra dimension to your shots. Always keep an eye out for features that make strong frames and keep a variety of shots on file for use in photographs where a good frame is lacking.

Elements or other software package. It beats having to rip off a branch and dangle it in front of the lens to hide an eyesore—an old pre-digital trick!

It is worth keeping a file of useful shots that can be employed at a later stage. Frames can often be found when the shot's actual subject matter is of little use. Using Photoshop Elements, it is possible to select the frame, cut it out, and use it in another shot. Take several shots with different focal lengths and angles so that a good choice is available.

You must remember to keep a balance between the foreground and the subject, so as not to make the frame too dominant in the

shot. Don't let the subject become too small by using your lens at too wide an angle. Instead, move back and use the middle range of your zoom lens to slightly compress the perspective, thus making the subject naturally bigger.

Depth of field can be altered to place emphasis on the frame or the background. A tree, for example, can be made the focal point and the background made out of focus using a telephoto and a large aperture, letting the shape of the tree dominate the shot. Alternatively, focusing on the background can make the tree out of focus, drawing the eye into the shot. Both can be kept in focus with a long exposure if a suitable support is available.

TIP Choose a frame with similar lighting, and with sunlight coming in from the same direction. You can always flip one of the images in Elements from left to right or vice versa.

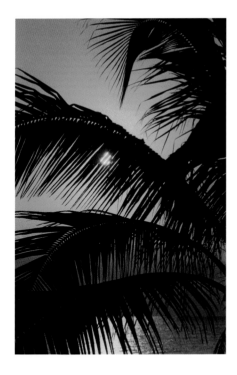

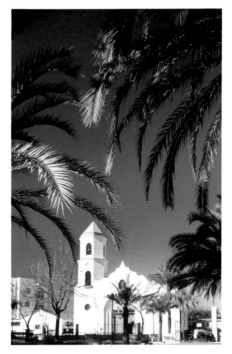

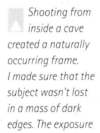

The palm leaves in this Florida sunset become both the frame and the subject of the picture at the same time. Again, I zoomed in for a tight crop, *which emphasizes the shapes of the leaf silhouettes. Meanwhile, careful positioning of the sun behind a leaf stopped flare from ruining the shot.*

The palm trees were used here to create a simple frame around the church. I chose the angle and moved backward behind the trees to place the *church carefully between two palm leaves. This takes thought at the time, but you'll get extra Brownie points for such careful attention to detail!*

Shooting from inside a cave created a naturally occurring frame. I made sure that the subject wasn't lost in a mass of dark edges. The exposure *of the sea was taken before entering the cave and was entered as a manual setting. I then bracketed several shots either side of this reading.*

Focal points

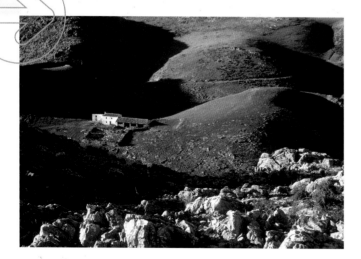

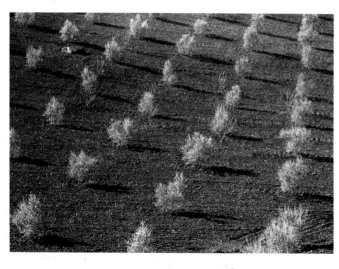

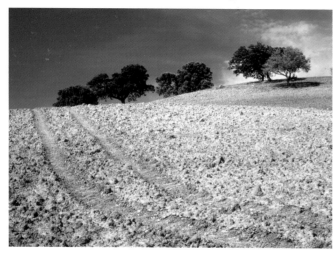

Most landscapes should have what is known as a focal point within the image. This is usually the subject and the main point of interest within the composition. Without a focal point most landscapes suffer from "wandering eye syndrome." That is, the eye wanders around the frame aimlessly trying to find some relevance to the shot.

The focal point in a shot is usually obvious—it is probably the thing that drew your attention to the shot in the first place. It may be an isolated group of trees in a desolate landscape, a farm on a hill, a boat on the sea, or a dramatic rock formation. It may even be a small element within the frame, but it will be strong enough to bind the whole composition together. The focal point often gives the picture a sense of scale. If you have a large expanse of sand, one tiny dot of a person can suddenly add meaning to the shot. By using all the other compositional aids, you can create strong dynamic shots time after time.

DETAIL

Don't forget that many lenses can focus down to a short distance. Often referred to as macro photography, this is a valuable ally. It allows a range of images taken at close (but not microscopic) distance. Many modern lenses can focus down to these levels, making it a shame to waste their potential.

Many details await the photographer in the world of macro. Although it is not a traditional landscape photograph as such, you should always keep an eye out for interesting shots. Close-ups of flowers can produce captivating images. Use minimal depth of field by opening up the aperture, and some beautiful shots can be achieved. The next step is to turn that fleeting sensation into a viable photograph.

Here the house is clearly the point of interest, but its diminutive size leaves you feeling how small mankind is compared to nature. Rocks have been used to create foreground interest leading the eye down to the farm.

Symmetrical patterns occur frequently in nature, but not usually in quite such a regimented form as these rows of trees. Any type of repetition can be an interesting subject to photograph. Good side lighting is often an essential requirement.

If this shot had been taken on a dull day, the effect would have been diluted considerably. The intense blue offsets the barren land perfectly. A small group of trees in the top third of the frame anchors the whole shot together.

Picking out detail from the general scene can simplify design and composition, letting you focus on one specific element. Placing your camera on a tripod enables you to let it wander around the scene. Focus and compose at leisure.

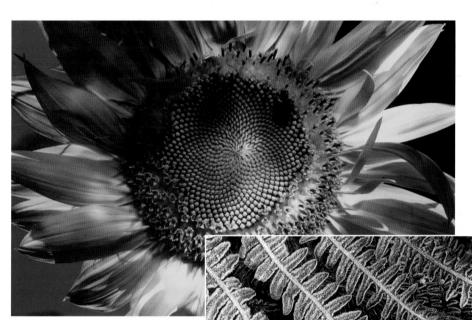

Getting in close to a subject can reveal new and often exciting areas of discovery. Nature is often revealed in its full glory when you zoom in close. Most lenses will have some form of macro ability—that is, the ability to focus very close to a subject. Check the camera for lens specs before you buy. Combine a wide focal range with the ability to focus closely and you can take advantage of various photographic opportunities.

TIP → Macro shots will suffer from even the slightest camera shake, just as long telephoto shots do. Both are highly magnified. Use a suitable support to avoid having them ruined by blurring.

It's always a good idea to look where you're walking! I nearly walked straight past this group of frozen bracken leaves. The frost has left a beautiful design all over the leaves. Getting in closer has helped to reveal this fine detail. A steady hand or tripod is a must to maintain the intricate patterns when printed.

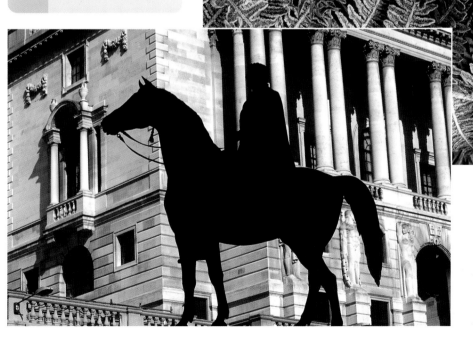

As the sun moved around, I saw the statue was going into shadow, letting me take the silhouette. I returned an hour later after taking some other shots.

Color

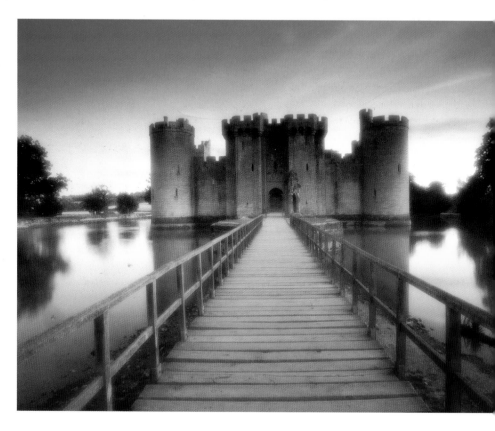

Color helps create atmosphere and sets the tone of the entire image—a funfair, for example, exudes many clashing, vibrant colors that compete for attention.

At the opposite end of the spectrum a moody, somber, misty winter sunrise may exhibit the merest hint of color and be almost monochromatic.

Knowing what to look for and how to take advantage of color is essential to creating a successful photograph.

Light creates color by absorbing certain wavelengths and reflecting others. All colors are made by mixing the three basic primary colors of red, blue, and green. A yellow sunflower, for example, absorbs blue light; the green and red light reflected make the color yellow.

This is also what happens at sunset when the sun is at a low angle and the atmosphere absorbs more blue light. Mixing equal amounts of all three will produce white light. Black is created when all colors are absorbed in equal amounts. Gray is also an equal amount of all three colors; a cool gray has a slight bias to the blue end of the spectrum. A TV monitor uses red, green, and blue phosphors.

Although it's great to find perfect shots, digital manipulation allows for some wonderful, varied, and precise effects to be achieved with minimal effort. Perfect digital color harmony (or discord!) is only a mouse click or two away.

Here the sunset has a single color range of reds, yellows, and oranges. It sends a clear, strong message about the warmth we associate with this end of the color spectrum.

Understanding colors and their relationships is fundamental to creating pictures with impact. The successful photographer will use the psychological effect of color intelligently by juxtaposing harmonious and/or complementary hues to create the right emotion. The warmer, more animated harmonies of red and yellow create a feeling of summer. Colder, more subdued blues and violets remind us of winter. These qualities can be used to alter the mood of a shot.

This diagram shows where each color lies on the color wheel. Clashing colors lie opposite each other while harmonious ones lie side by side.

The lovely cool blue sky above Bodiam Castle in England adds just the right amount of color tension to the contrasting warm wood and bricks.

Color is one of nature's greatest gifts. Each season brings with it a new way of seeing and using color to create form and structure in the landscape.

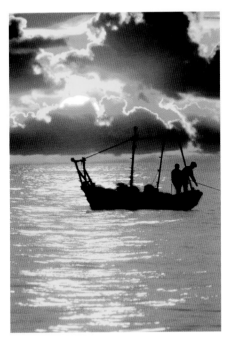

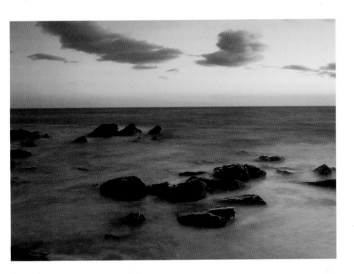

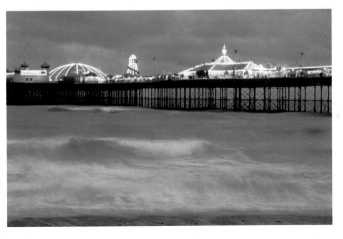

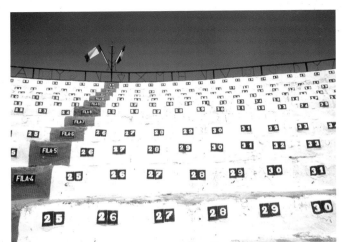

In this shot the sun has recently gone down, leaving the shoreline bathed in beautiful warm colors. Capturing these colors in low-light conditions takes a wide aperture and a long exposure, but the result gives the scene a stunning sense of atmosphere.

The cold blue color helps to set off the small amount of warm artificial tungsten lighting on this pier. The two contrasting colors create a disharmonious tension. In this case, the effect is subtle— the overall color is biased to the blue end of the spectrum.

This blue is totally different—it is the intense blue of a clear sunny day. The bright yet limited color palette has led to a graphic shot that would not have worked at all on a dull day. Remember: white objects need careful exposure—try 1½ to 2 stops over the suggested meter reading to be sure.

WARM COLORS

Reds, yellows, and oranges are very strong, dominant colors—the colors of summer. They are the colors of fun and life. Red is also the color of blood and a sign of danger, signifying the warmth of the sun and blazing fire. Because of this we perceive any object that is colored as being hot.

COLD COLORS

Blues, violets, and cyans are cold colors—the colors of winter. They are known as receding colors because the landscape gets cooler in color toward the horizon. This effect can be used to portray a feeling of depth when warmer colors are used in the foreground. Dawn is often cooler than sunset; adding a blue color cast to boost your shot will give a sense of tranquillity and calm. Cool colors create a sense of sadness and depression, which humans often feel when it's cold outside—hence the term "feeling blue."

Color

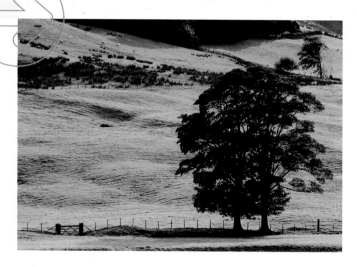

NATURAL COLORS

White is often associated with purity; it is what you might call a colorless color. White is all colors combined. Snow evokes a feeling of isolation, cold, and freshness, but is also used to give a modern feeling. Black, on the other hand, immediately creates a somber, sad feeling.

Because nature creates most living plants in green, this color is probably perceived as the most natural. It is nature's base color; the color of growth and fertility. Think of a field of fresh, cool green crops in spring and compare it to an empty hot arid desert. This is the power of color in action.

Chlorophyll, which creates the green color inside plants, is the building block of life on Earth. It has to be one of the most natural and important colors in life! This shot encapsulates Mother Nature's most popular color.

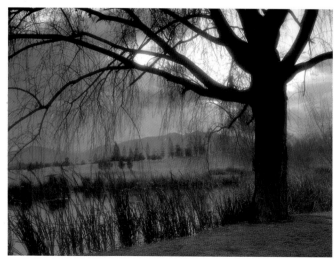

PASTEL COLORS

When colors are muted or desaturated, a pastel effect is created. Any colors can be used together quite successfully when muted. Fog and mist, for example, naturally help to desaturate and harmonize all colors. As we'll explain later in Chapter Three, image-editing applications, such as Adobe Photoshop Elements, allow excellent color control, so that even strong colors can be desaturated to create delicate color effects. If necesary, you can also make use of filters to bring a shot to life. Adding a little noise, for example, can help to create atmosphere.

The sunset didn't quite happen on this occasion as it clouded over. I persevered and still came away with a nice shot, although not the one I was expecting! The cool blue color is a natural phenomenon of overcast weather conditions in low light.

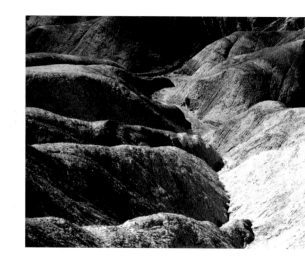

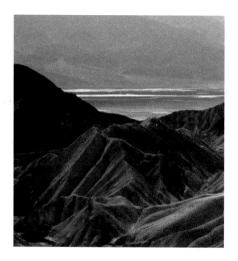

Here, in Death Valley, the temperature was formidable—it almost melted my camera! These are stark, almost monochromatic shots with minimal color. If you find yourself in similar circumstances, try using a polarizer to reduce heat haze and glare.

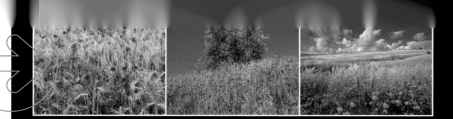

Color can be made to work in a whole variety of ways, depending on whether it is used aggressively, with great subtlety, or somewhere in between. In the right hands it will add mood, atmosphere, and power to a photograph.

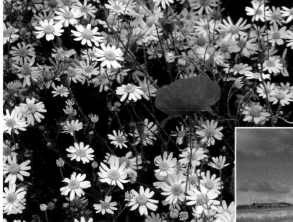

A single red poppy has the ability to dominate a shot even when it is quite small—such is the power of the color red.

The red swathe of poppies in this shot is quite dominant in the foreground. Add a dramatic sky and sun and you have a

winning visual combination. An ugly telegraph pole which would otherwise have ruined the shot was cloned out.

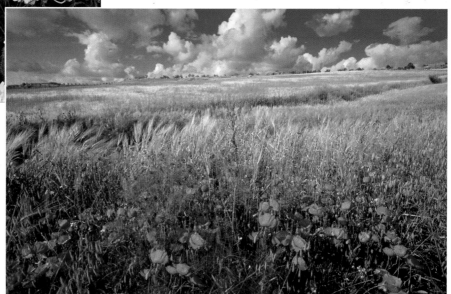

MONOCHROMATIC COLORS

Color photographs do not need to contain every color of the rainbow to convey mood. Using one dominant color with a secondary hue present can create an immediate and powerful effect. The narrowing of the visual spectrum lets the subject matter become more dominant. Shapes and form take on a more important role in the power of the final image. Silhouettes can also work very well with monochromatic colors as they let you create a graphic interpretation of the subject.

COMPLEMENTARY COLORS

Nature offers a world of color in many different forms. There are two basic types of color: complementary colors (yellow/violet, blue/orange, red/green), which are opposite each other on the color wheel; and harmonious colors, which lie next to each other on the color wheel. The primary colors red, green, and blue are mixed to make up the secondary colors of yellow, cyan, and magenta. By mixing equal quantities of red, green, and blue, white light is created.

Complementary colors give maximum contrast, creating a jarring sensation when used together. This can be used to eye-catching effect in a shot. By making one color more dominant in the picture, more subtle color-contrast effects can be produced.

HARMONIOUS COLORS

Colors that lie either side of each other on the color wheel are considered harmonious. This is why green when mixed with yellow and blue creates a harmonious effect. This is the color of a field of young green crops on a sunny day with a blue sky. A field of sunflowers is also harmonious, but if you darken the sky to a deep blue with a polarizing filter, you begin to get more contrast. This is because the blue begins to enter the violet/purple end of the spectrum, which is opposite to yellow on the color wheel.

FACT FILE

Color detail
Sometimes color can become the subject matter in a photograph. It may often be only a detail within a larger subject, so be prepared to tightly crop the composition. Removing the subject from its fuller context creates an abstract pattern, so be on the lookout for interesting textures and details within the wider picture. The telephoto end of your lens is ideal for capturing such shots.

Light

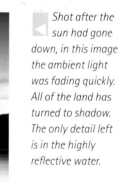

Shot after the sun had gone down, in this image the ambient light was fading quickly. All of the land has turned to shadow. The only detail left is in the highly reflective water.

This vantage point was reached in time to take a sunset. It was a moody affair that I tried to accentuate. It's difficult to fight the light, so go with the flow! A gray grad filter (see page 58) was used for an "end of the world" effect.

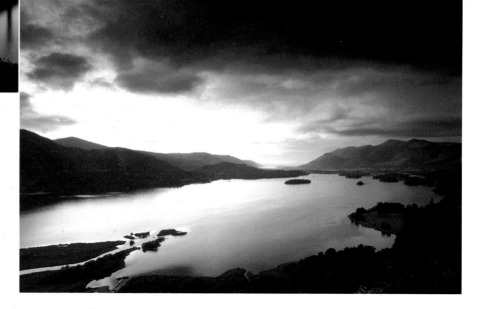

Capturing the ever-changing quality of light represents a unique challenge for the photographer. As the sun rises and sets, it is possible to capture a range of different moods and feelings. How you choose to harness Mother Nature's natural lighting rig is totally up to you.

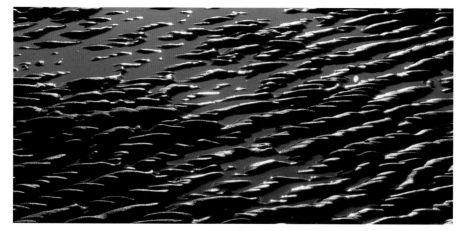

This low-key shot has hardly any highlight detail—just enough to show the texture and form of the sand. The sun was very low in the sky to get this shot. You do not want gray, so underexpose by 1 stop and then 1½ stops to keep the wonderful dark colors.

High-key shots are harder in landscapes because you don't have much control over the tones present in the land. Shooting in winter with snow on the ground helps to create a more high-key effect. You can alter the contrast range using Levels in Adobe Elements.

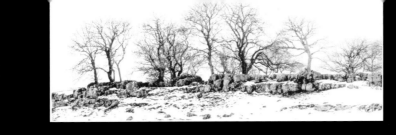

Undoubtedly light is the most important factor involved in a photograph. From the grandest vista to the smallest detail, light is the most valuable ally any photographer has.

Quality of light changes throughout the day and the seasons. It is also dependent on the weather conditions.

Early and late light creates the most drama. The strong directional side lighting is ideal for landscapes; it reveals texture, shape, and form. As the sun rises, it becomes harsher and more contrasting and you lose the shadows that add all the drama. Photographs are still possible, but look out for more graphic shots where color might play a more important role. Shooting in winter can give you the best light of all. Because the sun is low in the sky, you get fantastic side lighting all day long.

Weather is also an important factor. Shooting on an overcast day will yield soft directionless light. This is great for portraits, but less so for landscapes. It is a good time to try black-and-white shots, but some subjects such as flowers with delicate detail work well in softer light. Adding a little sun to a stormy gray day will result in very dramatic shots.

HIGH KEY/LOW KEY

Knowing how your exposure system works will let you create a specific style of shot. Altering the exposure, along with considered thought as to the subject matter of your photograph and the type of exposure to which it is suitable, can give rise to surprisingly different moods.

HIGH KEY

High-key photography makes use of a restricted tonal and color range. The image tends to portray a delicate, ethereal, two-dimensional quality and is predominantly made up of light tones. This should not be confused with a high-contrast image, which can include both pure black and pure white tones in the shot. A high-key image has a squashed tonal range of predominantly medium to light grays and whites.

The background should be bright and overexposed to add to the overall effect. It is often possible to combine elements of high key with those of high contrast, where the subject is predominantly made up of light colors, but there are small areas of dark tones in the shot.

Good subjects include landscapes and woodland scenes shot on misty days. The mist turns dark colors into pale colors. Combine the sun and a little overexposure and you can produce pleasing high-key landscape shots.

LOW KEY

Low-key photography produces completely the opposite feelings to high-key shots, but should not be confused with images that are low-contrast, which suffer from a lack of solid blacks. Low key is essentially a medium-to-high contrast image heavily biased toward a predominance of dark tones.

Dark, brooding, stormy landscapes lend themselves well to the low-key approach. Here, dark shadows and dark backgrounds help to create a shadowy, somber, mysterious feeling with a three-dimensional effect. Generally speaking, there is far more subject matter to choose from, because most shooting situations will be in the medium-to-high contrast zones ideally suited to low-key photography.

The painter Rembrandt was probably the greatest master of low-key studies, using a technique called chiaroscuro in which objects are brought out strongly by the use of a dark background that is highlighted by brighter areas. Low-key is essentially a medium-to-high contrast image heavily biased toward a predominance of dark tones.

There are no hard-and-fast rules to shooting high-key and low-key shots and many times you will find there is a cross-over with another style or technique. Use it as a starting point and get creative!

The soft diffused light has helped to create a high-key effect here. The computer was used to lighten the shot.

This has a monochromatic effect, where one color is dominant throughout the shot of the pier.

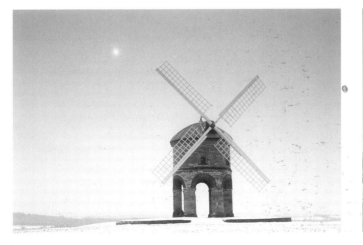

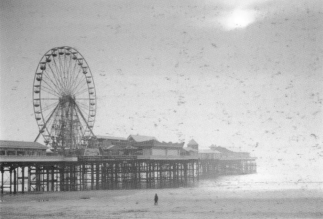

Time of day

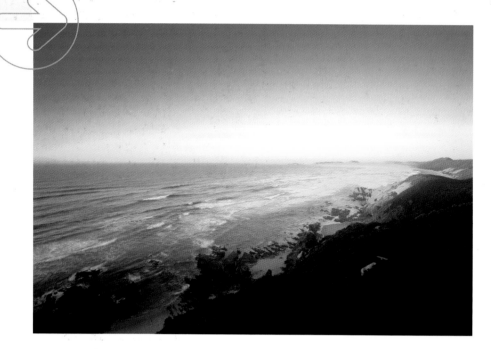

Venture out on a dull, dreary day and the chances are you will get dull, dreary, boring shots. The secret to great shots is to be in the right place at the right time. Get the mix of light and subject matter right and you will almost definitely be assured of a great photograph being exposed onto your CCD. Light is without doubt the photographer's most important tool. Knowing how and when to get the best out of the light will dramatically improve your shots overnight.

SUNRISE

This is the quietest part of the day when even the birds are not yet awake—if you can struggle out of bed in the middle of the night to be in position for daybreak, you will be rewarded with a tranquil yet inspiring experience. Weather is always the main bone of contention with landscape shots, so listening carefully to the weather report will give you an idea of what to expect. Pleasant weather conditions such as morning mist evaporating can create an unexpected atmospheric bonus.

As the night gives way to daybreak, a soft landscape begins to emerge, in which shadows are weak and colors are muted and pastel in hue. The light is often clean and clear and on the cool side because atmospheric haze and pollution are at their lowest. Many advertising shots are done in this period because the light is soft and sensuous. This sunless light minimizes contrast problems and is ideal for bringing out maximum detail.

As the dawn sun breaks over the horizon, the light changes very quickly. The world is flooded with soft warm light which races across the land, producing wonderful long shadows that create a 3-D effect and reveal texture and shape in the hills and valleys. In winter there are fantastic contrasts between cool blue shadows and warm red highlights, leading to some fantastic shots.

You will have about a 20-minute window of opportunity to grab light at its best, so you have to work fast and be in position or the moment will be lost. Your camera will also have to react because the exposure can change within seconds by several f-stops. Always keep an eye on the exposure and verify it for every shot you take. If you're shooting into the sun, remember to take the reading without the sun in the shot or underexposure will occur.

Sunrise is harder to work out where to position yourself than sunset, as you don't have the sun setting to give an approximation of where the light will strike first as it appears. Using a compass will give an idea of which way is east, but revisiting a good beauty spot is well worthwhile as intimate knowledge of the area will always help when scouting for the best spots.

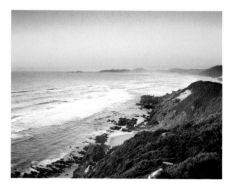

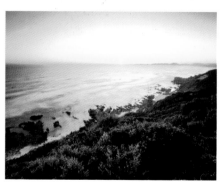

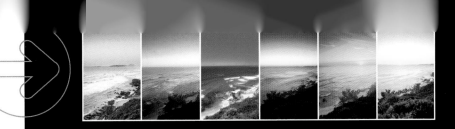

The quality of light changes considerably during the day—from soft muted colors at sunrise , through harsh midday sunlight, back to soft colors at sunset. It also changes in color, contrast, strength, and direction as the sun tracks through the sky.

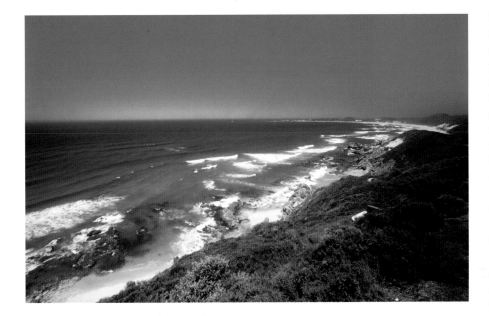

Early morning and early evening are ideal for landscape shots. In the time after sunrise and before sunset the warm, muted colors and soft light bring out the best from the scene.

The harsh light of midday maximizes contrast and pushes color saturation to the limit. With a strong scene and a simple, bold composition, this is still a good time to shoot.

MIDDLE OF THE DAY

Many photographers pack up for the day after shooting the sunrise, as the light becomes harsher and more contrasting. Although most landscapes work best at sunrise or sunset, good images can still be found. Colors are now fully saturated, especially with a polarizing filter, and the light is at its hardest with short featureless shadows. On these occasions the secret is to look for shots that these lighting conditions will enhance. Simple shots containing few elements work best. Although not set in stone, the old adage of shooting with the sun behind you often works best for maximum color and graphic intensity.

LATE AFTERNOON/SUNSET

Like early morning, this is a good time for shooting landscapes—especially in an urban environment where buildings will benefit from strong side lighting. It is often called the Golden Hour—the sunlight has warmed up again as it descends to the horizon. The hour before sunset gives you perhaps the best part of the day. Shooting into the sun can give dramatic foreground silhouettes depending on the sun's intensity, but remember: don't look directly into the sun, especially through a telephoto lens, as eyes can be damaged. If possible, stop down the lens with a depth-of-field button or use sunglasses. A gray graduated filter is often useful to maintain a balance between sky and land. Even a digital camera has limitations to the amount of detail it can record.

DUSK/TWILIGHT

Don't pack up your camera just yet! Many interesting shots are to be had after the sun has disappeared. You now get the beautiful soft afterglow of dusk when the light is still glowing with warmth—very similar to the light of pre-dawn. Long exposures can turn the sea

into an ethereal mist, while cities come alive. Watch the change in the mix of artificial and natural light happen over a half-hour period and keep on shooting every five minutes. In this case, dusk shots usually work much better than dawn shots because there are no lights on in the houses early in the morning. Keep shooting, using long exposures until the sky has gone black. A dark blue tint in the sky often compliments the warm colors of artificial lighting.

COLOR TEMPERATURE

Measured in degrees kelvin, this is the scale by which color is measured.

As the sun rises, its color changes and this can be measured. Normal daylight is measured at 5,500° K—this is when the sun is around the middle of the day and colors reflected off objects are deemed to be normal (i.e., a white object appears white with no color cast). If you photograph at sunset, the temperature drops to about 2,500° K, which is a redder color. The white object will now reflect a red color. The human brain does a very good job of cancelling out this color change, but the camera's CCD records a true image. The scene, therefore, will look warmer than you remember. This is generally not a bad thing, but you can alter the white balance to correct this if necessary. Such color casts can be a problem if you are photographing inside a tungsten-lit room and you want the colors to look normal.

Different light sources also emit strong color casts—mercury vapor lights are green and sodium lights are yellow. On the whole, it is best to correct any casts introduced in your image-editing software (*see page 84-91*).

> **TIP** If you're shooting into the sun, take an exposure reading without the sun in shot— or your picture will be underexposed.

Contre jour

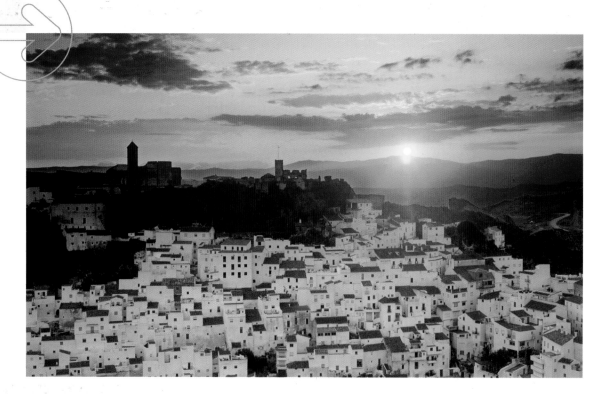

In this shot a gray grad filter (see page 58) was used to maintain detail in the white village. The village still needed to be brightened and the contrast was also boosted to balance the shot. Without the gray grad the village would have disappeared into a black shadow.

"Contre jour" is a fancy French term that simply means "shooting into the light." This technique cannot be achieved without some form of dramatic light, which you use to create moody, atmospheric shots. Create silhouettes by shooting into the light. For this you have to expose to allow for the bright light to turn any foreground interest into dark shadow. When the shape of an object is reduced to its bare outline, the resulting silhouette can create a fantastic graphic form. It really helps to bring out the profile of objects. This technique can transform ordinary-looking subjects into really strong visual statements.

Using reflectors or flash for fill-in light can give you the best of both worlds. Here you should choose a more detailed shot for your subject matter, as fill-in light has limited power, so large areas of landscape can't be lit properly. Backlight the subject as usual and use fill-in during the exposure. A reflector is an ideal means of reflecting light back into the subject because you can see the effect before pressing the shutter. Flash requires more experience and generally gives a less natural lighting effect.

Exposing for silhouettes is relatively easy. Most cameras actually produce perfect exposures by mistake. The exposure meter is fooled into underexposure by an overly bright dominant light source, which is exactly what you want. The severity of underexposure that you will need also depends on your subject. Strong shapes such as trees or buildings work well going completely black, but some, such as flower details, require bracketing to find the best exposure. Other subjects such as sunsets require you to override this exposure for correctly exposed shots.

One potential problem with this technique is lens flare. This is caused by light reflecting off internal glass elements within the zoom. Try to hide the sun behind your subject to reduce possible flare. When shooting backlit trees, for example, a single branch can be used. There is a fine line between flare and the starburst effect, where specular highlights turn into little stars. The lens diaphragm being stopped down causes this. With the sun behind a tree branch, try moving your camera a fraction and the tiny amount of controlled sunlight will turn into a starburst effect. In other instances, flare can be used creatively. Pixel-based software such as Adobe Photoshop Elements actually has its own lens flare filter to do the job in a controlled manner. Although bad flare is very difficult to retouch on the computer, small dots of flare can be eradicated quite successfully with the Clone tool.

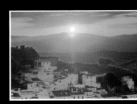
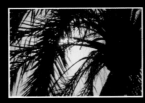

Backlighting your subject lets you create instant graphic images where the shape of the subject is important to the final impact of the shot. Using a gray grad filter lets you keep detail in the shadows.

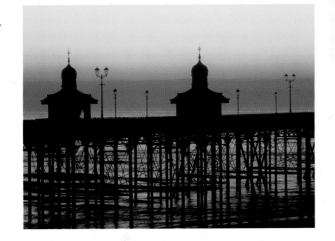

A classic silhouette where strong backlighting has rendered the pier a solid black. Simply meter from the sky to create this type of effect. Use the Levels command to fine-tune the mid-tone and highlights later on before printing the picture.

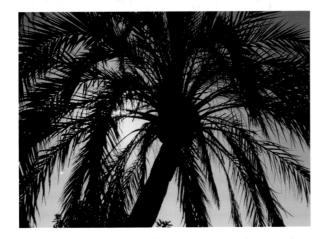

If shooting with the sun directly in the frame, try to partially hide it behind the subject to avoid bad lens flare problems. With the sun directly behind the palm tree, the camera has automatically underexposed the image creating a silhouette.

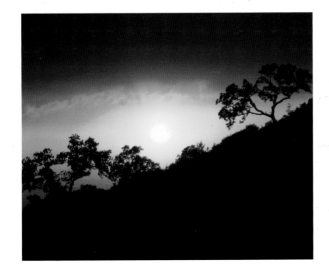

This is taken from the series of shots made at one of my favorite sunsets in Spain. The sun is partially hidden behind cloud, so didn't flare too much in this shot. A meter reading was taken to the side of the frame to ensure that the bright sun didn't influence the meter into underexposing.

FACT FILE

Contre jour with landscapes

Shooting into the light can also produce dramatic wide-angle landscapes. The sun may pop out from behind a cloud during a storm to light the land. Here you may want to retain a balance between land and sky, so, if possible, use a gray grad filter to maintain detail in shadows and highlights. It may also pay dividends to shoot several exposures for highlights and shadows when the lighting and subject matter are very complicated. Use Photoshop Elements to put the shots in *Layers* and use the *Eraser* tool to get rid of darker or lighter areas.

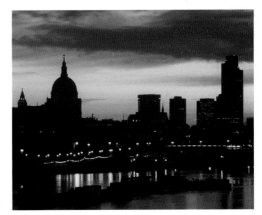

This was shot very early one summer's morning at 4 a.m. London was fast asleep, apart from one person who called the police saying I was up to no good at that time in the morning on

Waterloo Bridge! Fortunately I was rewarded with a great sky for all my troubles. Notice how the office buildings aren't lit up at this time, and the different feel this gives to a cityscape.

Sunrise and sunset

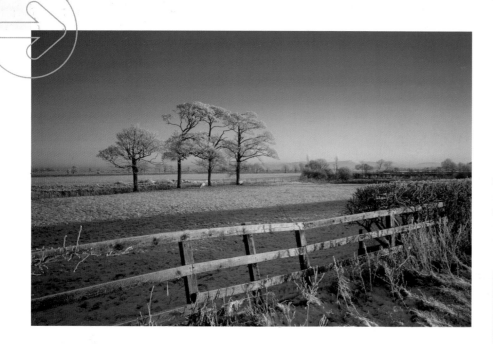

For this shot, a pre-dawn start let me to take full advantage of the amazing hoar frost. I normally drive past these trees, but not this time—they looked fantastic. Unusual weather can make mundane sites seem special.

Shooting on cloudless days can lead to disappointing results, but a little mist or haze can lead to a beautiful pale orange sun hanging in the sky. You will need an interesting foreground subject to give more impact to the shot on such occasions.

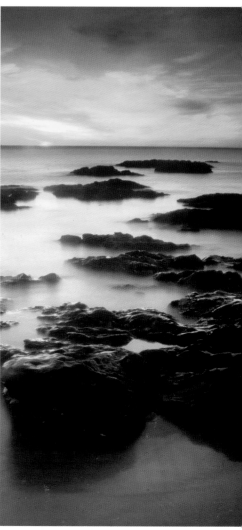

There is nothing quite so breathtaking as a sunrise or sunset caught in its full glory. But catching it is not simply a matter of point and click—it takes time, patience, and planning to keep pace with the sun. The photographer who is able to follow a few straightforward rules will be rewarded many times over.

Here the rocks and clouds have combined to create a strong composition. They almost mirror each other—the soft and hard textures of nature. The soft light of dusk also adds to the rich textures.

For the photographer, the most interesting light occurs in a narrow band just before and just after sunset or sunrise. Perhaps the most magical moment is when the sun is just about to appear from below the horizon or is just about to disappear for the day. The sun is at its lowest and casts wonderful long shadows, and where the sun hits water, it creates a long shimmering beam of golden light.

Sunrise is a much quieter affair than sunset. Often, the land is eerily still, without even the birds moving or making any noise. It is usually colder because the land has cooled down during the night. In good weather conditions you will either be greeted with crystal-clear light or mist and fog formed during the night. Clouds are a godsend as they add lots of drama to the sky, and will take on the beautiful fiery colors of the sun when it is just above or below the horizon. Take plenty of shots as the sun and clouds interact. The light and color will change continuously, so be ready.

Sunsets are warmer, due to more pollution and haze being present in the sky at the end of the day. Clouds are also more interesting and livelier as the sun has warmed them up over the day, producing faster-flowing and more changeable formations.

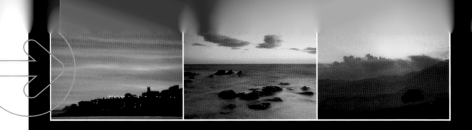

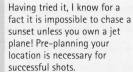

Getting up from a warm cosy bed at the crack of dawn is difficult, especially in the winter, but it can lead you to some of your most memorable photographic experiences and one or two memorable shots in the bag as well.

Shooting with a telephoto, I just managed to grab the last remnants of the sun going down. The sun sets remarkably quickly when you stop and time it. You have to be able to set up your shot quickly if you arrive on the scene late.

The breakwater jutting out into the sea, the pebbles in the foreground, and the slow shutter speed have made

this shot. The breakwater creates tension within the composition, being placed at an angle to the horizon.

TIP Having tried it, I know for a fact it is impossible to chase a sunset unless you own a jet plane! Pre-planning your location is necessary for successful shots.

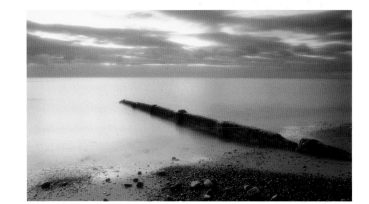

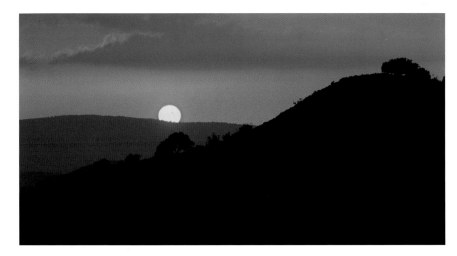

This was shot while with my parents in Marbella, Spain. I'm glad I remembered to take my camera and tripod

along! It needed several seconds' exposure, which would not have been possible with a hand-held camera.

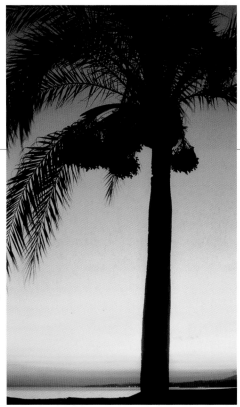

FACT FILE

Silhouettes

Making a silhouette with a sunset is easy. Most foreground subject matter will automatically come out jet-black in these conditions because the camera's meter will underexpose when there is such a bright-point light source.

Silhouettes can produce very strong graphic images that look great blown up

big and framed on the wall. To keep detail, try using a gray grad filter over the sky and take a meter reading to the side of the sun so that it isn't in the frame. Keep an eye out for strong shapes that will work well as silhouettes. Look out for bold, simple lines that are going to be immediately recognizable.

Night photography

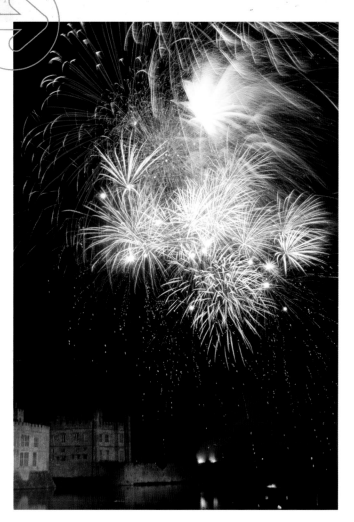

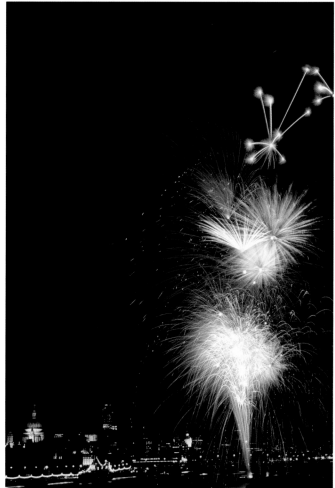

Night is one of my favorite times: you've just taken a great sunset, then you wait for light levels to fall for a night shot. Two for the price of one—my kind of deal!

Fireworks are a great subject — technically they are a little demanding, but good fun to shoot. A tripod is absolutely essential for success as exposures are quite long. Some foreground interest can help to balance the shot and show where the event took place.

Any camera and lens will suffice, but a tripod is an absolute must for successful night shots. You might think of night as a black sky, but the real secret to good photographs is to shoot at twilight. Also known as the crossover period, it is the time when light and color are still in the sky, but the sun has gone and any artificial illumination starts to become visible.

Find a subject such as an old building that is properly lit and you have hit the jackpot with almost guaranteed success. The best technique is to choose one location and shoot it over the entire twilight period until there is no color left in the sky. This will let you see how the mix of light affects the overall picture. As it gets darker and the exposure gets longer, very bright buildings can cause hot spots that will severely overexpose or "burn out." Shooting at shorter exposures to compensate will underexpose the sky and shadows to black, which usually looks awful. It is difficult to predict with accuracy the optimum point when all the different light sources are in balance, so keep on shooting!

One technique to try is to merge several shots together on the computer, steal the highlights from a bright building and put them in a shot where the general exposure is fine except for the burnt-out highlights. Exposures for night shots are not difficult. Use the average camera exposure as a starting point. Then bracket your exposures, as camera meters can be fooled into underexposure.

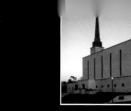
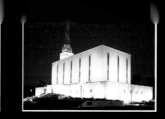

These two shots were taken within 15 minutes of each other, and highlight how important it is to keep shooting for as long as you can. Don't put the camera away until the sky has gone pitch black.

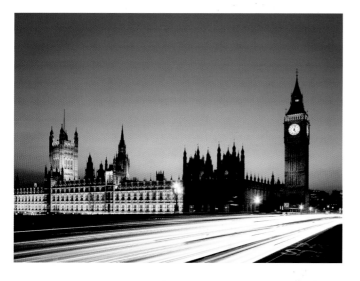

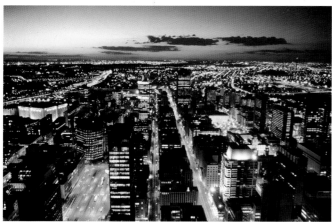

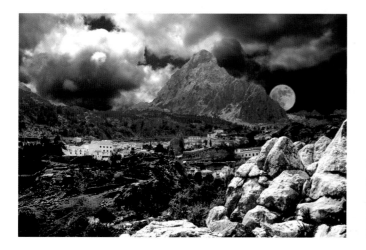

ACCESSORIES

Some form of cable release is essential, as trying to hold down the exposure button by hand for 30 seconds will usually result in camera shake ruining the shot.

COLOR CASTS

Color casts are common with night shots, as there is a multitude of different artificial lights. Although these can be corrected by camera filtration, it is easier to use Adobe Elements. On the whole most shots won't need correcting, as it is this very mix of color that adds to the flavor of the shot.

EXPERIMENTING

Try photographing urban neon signs with a zoom burst. This creates wonderful streaks of colored light radiating out from the center. An exposure greater than five seconds will work—too short and you won't have time to finish zooming. This is a somewhat hit-and-miss affair so take lots of shots with different shutter speeds and vary the zoom.

The traffic trails (top) were deliberately included to add to the drama of the shot. They also helped to hide an otherwise boring road.

Get up high (center) for a great shot. Look out for buildings with public access.

This started life as a daytime shot (below). Altering the contrast and color and adding a moon turned it into a pseudo-Hollywood image. In the cinema a dark blue filter was traditionally used to simulate night.

FACT FILE

Photographing by moonlight

Photographing the moon is a challenge. Shooting during a full moon will increase your chances, but good shots are possible with the moon in all its different phases. The main problem is that the moon overexposes very quickly, as it is so bright in comparison to the land. Also, an exposure greater than 10 seconds causes the moon to blur as it moves across the sky. It can be wiser to use an image-editing program to remove the blurred moon and replace it with an image shot separately. Shoot the moon at the longest setting on your lens and use a tripod to maintain maximum sharpness. If your camera has a spot facility, take a reading from the moon and bracket several exposures around it.

Movement and shutter speeds

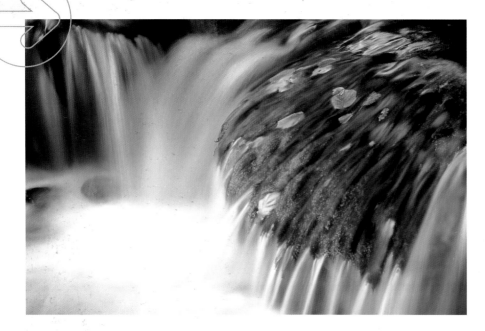

This close-up detail of a rock in a river was taken with an exposure of 10 seconds in dull lighting conditions. The duller the conditions, the easier it is to produce long exposures without resorting to neutral density filters. You can use the top half of a gray grad as a neutral density filter.

Capturing movement is dependent on aperture size and shutter speed. Don't be put off by the technical aspects of this subtle craft—even a rudimentary understanding of movement will let you create breathtaking images.

A photograph can be radically altered by the shutter speed that you choose for capturing the image. Long shutter speeds allow moving elements within the shot to blur for effect, while short, fast shutter speeds allow the subject to be frozen so that more detail can be seen. It depends on the mood and style that you wish to convey to your viewer. Long shutter speeds give a more ethereal mood, while faster shutter speeds let you focus on a particular subject, bringing it into sharper focus within the photo. A field of wheat can look soft and sensuous with a long shutter speed, or stark and well-defined with a short shutter speed.

LONG SHUTTER SPEEDS

When I first started to take an interest in photography I remember seeing shots of the sea that looked as though the water had turned to mist. It seemed as though they had been shot on another planet. Of course, I now know that it was merely a special technique that caused the blurring effect.

The effect was created by a simple technique by which you extend the shutter speed, so that the exposure takes full seconds rather than fractions of a second. A tripod, or at least a solid support such as a wall, is vital for long shutter speeds. Without it you will end up with camera shake, which will completely ruin the shot unless the effect is intentional (see *Motion Blur filter effects on page 82*).

Most of the time, long shutter speeds are easily achieved: you just stop down the lens to produce a sufficiently long exposure. In some circumstances, you may find that the ambient light levels are so bright that slow shutter speeds cannot be achieved, even when the lens is fully stopped down. In this case, a polarizer or neutral grad filter is needed to reduce the light levels for a sufficiently long exposure. Using a filter also allows a larger aperture to be used, giving a narrower depth of field.

FAST SHUTTER SPEEDS

Although slower speeds are the norm for landscape work, you may on occasion need a fast shutter speed to freeze your subject. One particular subject that springs to mind is flowers. I always keep an eye out for detail within the landscape and often it is the color and beauty of flowers that catches my attention. As flowers will sway even in the lightest breeze, a fast shutter speed becomes essential in order to freeze them in mid-sway. The obvious choice for increasing shutter

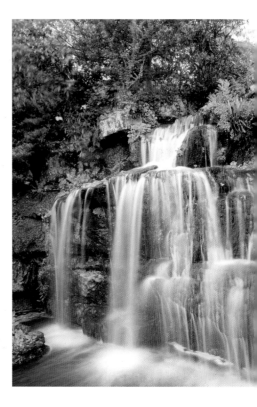

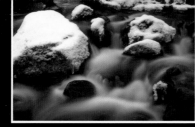

Shooting on a dull day without adding any orange warm-up color correction filters will often result in a very strong blue color cast. This is perfect for cold wintry shots. A soft-focus filter has softened the image slightly.

speed is to open up your lens aperture. This increases the amount of light getting to the CCD chip, thus allowing a faster shutter speed to be chosen. Naturally, wider apertures mean less depth of field, so there is always an ongoing battle between shutter speed for faster speeds and the aperture for extra depth of field. Often, a compromise has to be sought, but it is useless having good depth of field if the subject matter is blurred due to too long an exposure. In such an event, you have to forget depth of field concerns in order to capture the subject sharply. Thankfully, in many cases—especially with flowers—limited depth of field can actually accentuate the subject. I often try out a number of shutter speeds and see which one gives the best mixture between sharpness and depth of field.

One technique to try is using fill-in flash, which freezes the subject and may allow a longer shutter speed for better depth of field.

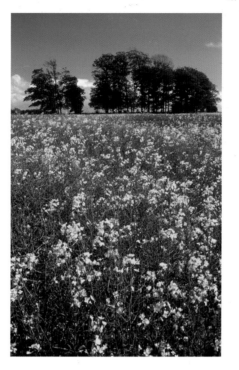

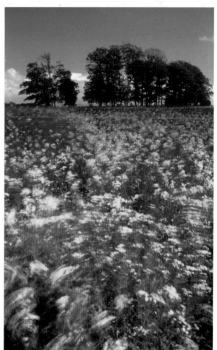

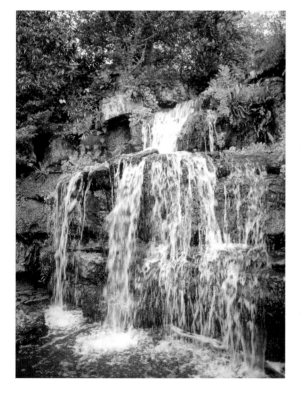

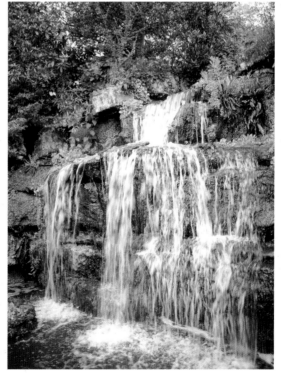

I normally shoot when there is a gap in the wind that stops everything from moving, but you can also use the wind to create deliberate blur effects. This works especially well with flowers and crops.

Shot at different shutter speeds (4 secs, 1/2 sec, 1/30 sec), this series of shots shows how the shutter speed affects flowing water during an exposure. Always try various shutter speeds to get a variety of effects.

Lens filters

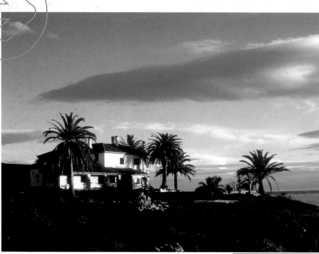

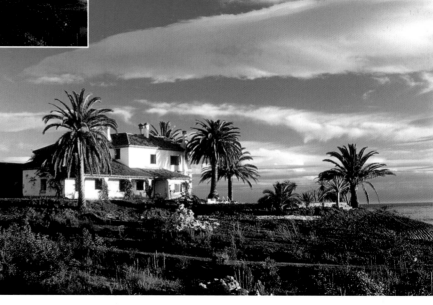

These two images graphically show the effect of a polarizing filter. In the shot below, the polarizing filter has made the sky much more dramatic. The sky itself is a much deeper blue color, while the clouds have increased contrast.

Many digital photographers may be surprised by my allegiance to traditional lens filters. True, a lot can be done using the filters in a software package, but some effects are only possible using on-camera filters. These are placed in front of the lens before the shot is taken. A little extra care and the thoughtful use of filters at the shooting stage can save unnecessary corrections later on.

TIP
Always shoot with the sun at a 90° angle to your camera for maximum polarization of the light to occur.

POLARIZING FILTER

The polarizing filter is without doubt the most important filter you can use. Its effect is truly magical, and it can transform a picture with a simple twist of the filter.

The polarizing filter polarizes the light that reflects off most non-metallic objects. Light travels in many directions and the polarizer prevents certain wavelengths from passing through to the lens. This reduces glare and haze, which in turn increases the clarity and color saturation of your shot.

Glare is also eliminated so that shiny surfaces such as windows and water will lose any reflections in them and darken in tone. Beautiful Mediterranean seas will turn transparent, making boats seem as if they are floating in mid-air. The maximum effect occurs when the filter is at a 45° angle to the reflection. These effects are impossible to re-create on the computer.

The biggest drawback with the polarizer is that it reduces the light that reaches your CCD sensor by two stops. In bright conditions this is not a worry, but you will need to use longer exposures and a tripod for lower light levels. Polarizers are made in two types: circular and linear. Both do exactly the same job but are intended to accommodate different designs in camera exposure meters. You may have to do some research to find out which one will work on your camera.

GRAY GRADUATE FILTER

This is a very important filter and should be in your camera bag along with the polarizer. The gray graduate (or gray grad) is primarily used for balancing the light levels of the sky and land. It has a graduated gray neutral-density color that fades to clear plastic half-way down. Skies are often several f-stops brighter than the land and without filtration you end up with a washed-out sky if you expose for the land, or a dark landscape if you expose for the sky. Smaller cameras may need a special filter holder to use a gray grad correctly.

NEUTRAL-DENSITY FILTER

A neutral-density filter is useful for deliberately reducing the light entering the camera to allow a longer shutter speed to be used. Longer shutter speeds can be used creatively to add motion in water. They are only needed if the light levels are so bright that your smallest aperture is still giving too fast a shutter speed. Try combining a neutral density and polarizer for really long exposures.

ULTRAVIOLET FILTER

This is normally the only screw-on filter that you will need to buy. Its effect is difficult to gauge but it cuts down UV, which can turn images shot in high-altitude places to blue. The filter's main benefit is that it acts as a high-quality protective cover for your expensive lens. A UV filter costs only a fraction of a new front lens element and protects against anything that can ruin a camera lens.

SOFT-FOCUS FILTER

A soft-focus effect can be applied to just about any subject in any lighting with great success. It should not be confused with an out-of-focus image. Although very nice effects can be made with Adobe Photoshop Elements using the *Gaussian Blur* filter, they will not replicate the effect that a soft-focus filter has when placed in front of the lens.

The lens filter creates a radiant glow around the edge of the highlights. It bleeds into the shadows and makes them slightly lighter. This effect is very difficult to achieve on the computer; a low-cost filter can give your shots a different creative avenue to go down. There are hundreds of soft-focus filters available, but you can also easily create your own filter. Use transparent cellophane, plastic self-adhesive tape, nylon stockings, or simply breathe on the lens.

When shooting, use a wide aperture, as small apertures will lessen the effect. Also, try overexposing to enhance the glow, and shoot your subject with a dark background so that the edges glow more·prominently.

FACT FILE

Filter holders and filter types

Owners of digital SLRs can attach filters as they would to a normal SLR. For other digital camera designs, you may need a specific lens or filter adaptor in order to use them. Filters come in many different designs. Screw-on filters attach directly to your lens and often remain there. Others are small thin rectangular plastic sheets that slide into a special holder, or are held over the lens by hand.

A filter holder attaches to the front of your lens and lets you slide the filters into place. You can rotate the holder to any angle and position the filter to any given point, making it a very useful piece of kit to have in your camera bag.

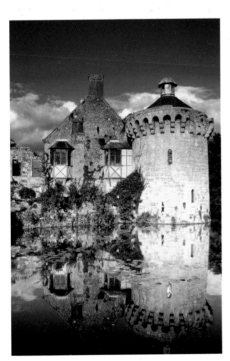

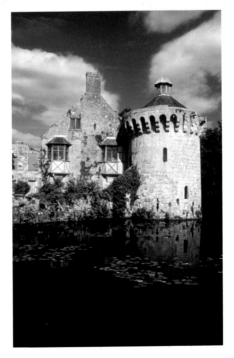

These two shots show the effectiveness of using a gray graduate filter in front of the lens. Some people argue that corrections to density can be done later on, but if shadow detail isn't picked up by the original camera exposure, then this becomes impossible.

Weather

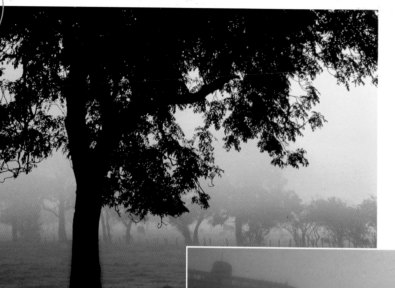

One of the biggest obstacles a photographer has to overcome is the weather. If luck is on your side, the weather can provide drama and atmosphere by the bucketful. If you get no luck, however, then you may be packing your bags and going home early. The weather has the potential to be your greatest friend or worst enemy. It is the one underlying ingredient that binds the whole image together to bring success or failure.

MIST AND FOG

One of the most interesting weather conditions that you can experience is mist or fog. Most of us wouldn't dream of venturing out on cold, wet, misty days, but you are depriving yourself of one of nature's most ethereal and magical weather conditions. Adverse weather conditions often produce far more interesting shots than those achieved on sunny days with a bland blue sky and featureless light.

Sometimes, if you get up early enough, you will witness mist forming in the valley bottoms or on lakes. If the sun happens to shine, the resulting interplay of light and vapor can produce beautiful

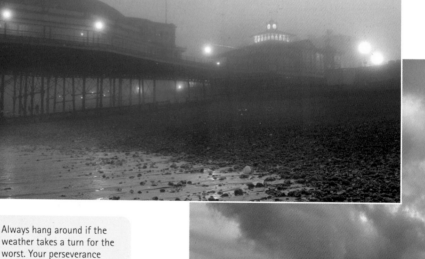

TIP Always hang around if the weather takes a turn for the worst. Your perseverance is often rewarded with atmospheric and moody shots.

Dawn is often a good time to find mist, as the cold air has settled on the ground during the night. This was shot with a telephoto lens to emphasize one foreground tree against the misty background. Mist and fog can produce some great backdrops, which let you place greater emphasis on your subject.

It had started off sunny the day this shot was taken, but then a sea mist suddenly rolled up out of nowhere. Most people pack up their bags and leave in these conditions, but I stayed on to get some really atmospheric and unusual shots showing the pier shrouded in mist.

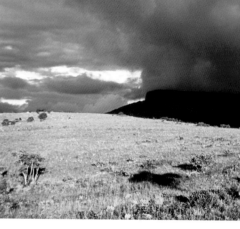

This wide-angle shot was actually created from several different pictures, montages together in Photoshop Elements. This is only the beginning of what you can do in your software.

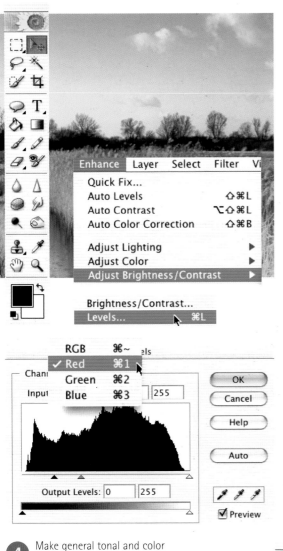

6 Remove any unsightly blemishes from your shot using the *Clone Stamp* tool (*see page 79*).

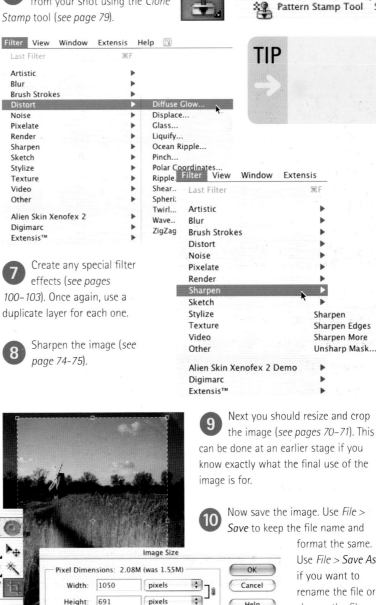

7 Create any special filter effects (*see pages 100-103*). Once again, use a duplicate layer for each one.

8 Sharpen the image (*see page 74-75*).

9 Next you should resize and crop the image (*see pages 70-71*). This can be done at an earlier stage if you know exactly what the final use of the image is for.

10 Now save the image. Use *File > Save* to keep the file name and format the same. Use *File > Save As* if you want to rename the file or change the file format from, say, a Photoshop PSD file to a Web-friendly JPEG file format.

4 Make general tonal and color adjustments using the *Levels* command (*see page 88*). At this stage, if you are happy with the result, you may duplicate this layer and throw away the original background layer.

5 Make selective local adjustments to color and tone using the selection tools: the *Rectangular Marquee*, *Lasso* tool, *Magic Wand*, and others.

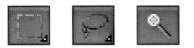

TIP

Cropping

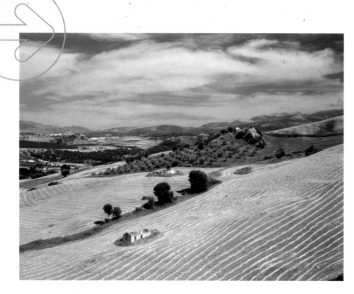

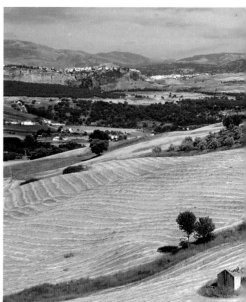

In this case the Spanish landscape shot was given a completely different feel by cropping out unwanted sky and land. Cropping can be used to make effective panoramic style formats.

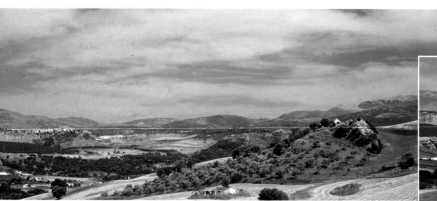

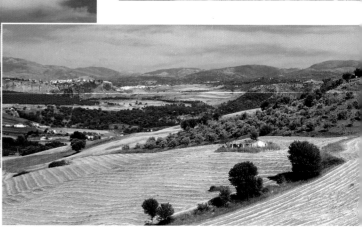

Cropping helps to bring order to a shot from a potentially confusing scene. The secret to good cropping is placing the objects within the frame to complement and enhance the main subject. Getting it right isn't always easy in situ, although with a bit of practice a zoom lens should let you fine-tune your compositions to a precise degree. Even bad shots can be rescued, thanks to the imaging power of your computer.

In the first crop I attempted to place emphasis on the sky. It may have been a good crop to choose for an image with a more dramatic sky with a bold silhouetted foreground, but here it didn't feel right.

Cropping an image is an easy way to improve a photograph. Most diehard photographers will argue that it should always be done in-camera, but I believe that a bit of a "tuck and snip" later on does no harm. None of us is perfect or so quick as to capture a scene flawlessly every time. A hastily taken shot with a wonky horizon is an easily forgivable offence. You may even have a fixed focal-length lens on your camera, so zooming to crop unwanted detail is not an option. If you can't get in as close as you want, due to a fixed lens or a small telephoto range on your zoom, walk up as close as you can to the subject and crop the rest off later.

I liked the second crop, but it didn't show the ruined farmhouse, which is what initially drew me to the shot in the first place.

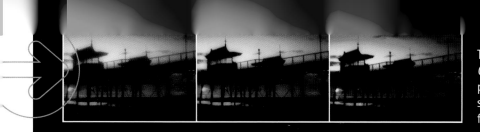

The *Gaussian Blur* filter (*Filter > Blur > Gaussian Blur*) adds extra mood to this pier shot. If you are looking for a softened effect, it is the perfect partner for using with blend modes.

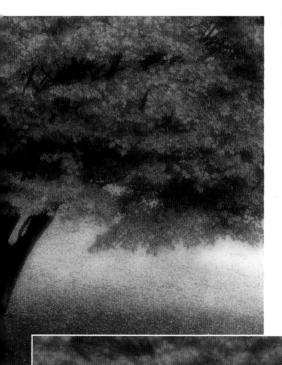

Blending layers

By experimenting with blend modes you can create some beautiful color effects, as you can see from this example. Run through the options in the *Layers* palette's pop-out menu. Be warned —experimenting with effects is addictive!

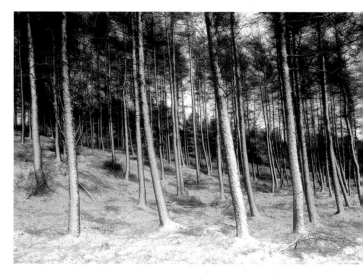

For this image, the background layer was copied and blurred using the Gaussian Blur filter.

I then chose Pin Light blend mode and a 61% Opacity to reduce the effect. I copied this layer again and this time I chose Saturation blend mode and an Opacity of 100%.

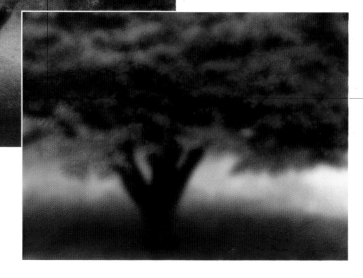

This is a combination of the Darken and Luminosity blend modes. A Luminosity layer above the Darken layer puts back the highlights that the Darken blend mode removes, giving you the best of both worlds.

I created five layers, all using the Luminosity blend mode, and flattened them. A lot of fine detail was destroyed, but it created a soft dreamy image that I rather like.

Soft-focus and motion blur

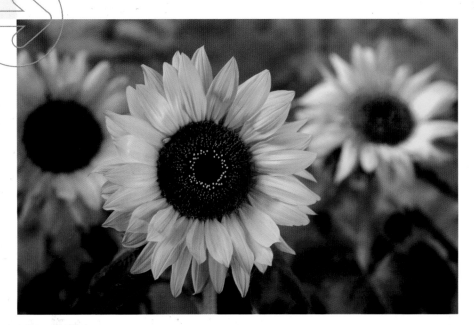

① For these images, the main sunflower was carefully selected using the *Magic Wand* and *Lasso* selection tools. The selection was saved and feathered by 2 pixels, and the sunflower remained selected for all the blur effects. This group of images demonstrates how the action of feathering your selection softens the pixels to produce a smooth mask edge.

② Below, I used an *Angle* of 45° to create a diagonal blur effect to add tension to the image. The *Distance* was set to 355 pixels to give a moderately strong result.

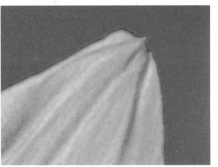

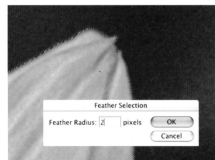

The *Motion Blur* effect and landscape photography might seem like an incongruous pairing, but in fact the *Motion Blur* filters can add a softening, impressionistic, or even dynamic quality to the subject matter. In these examples I've used the *Motion Blur* and its close cousin the *Radial Blur*—in both *Radial* and *Zoom* mode.

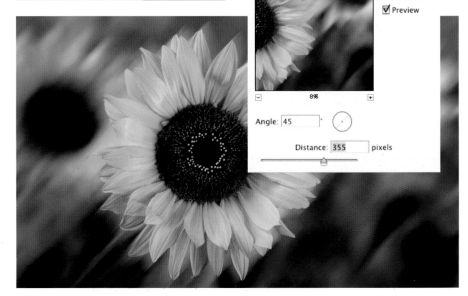

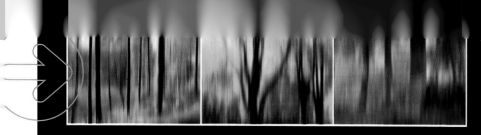

Use the *Motion Blur* filter on colorful images to create beautiful abstracts like these. Strong, geometric shapes like trees work really well.

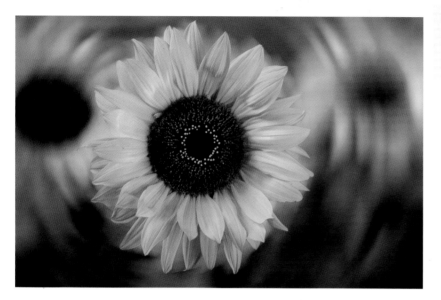

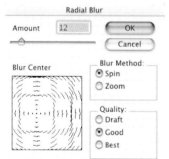

3 For this example, I applied the *Radial Blur* effect to the same image. The blur was moved slightly off-center so that the effect radiated around the main flower. The effect resembles ripples in a pond.

4 This is the sunflower image with the *Radial Blur* effect in *Zoom* mode. The blur center was again offset slightly.

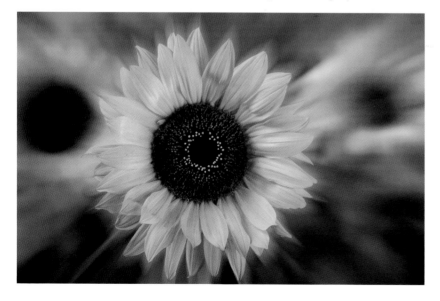

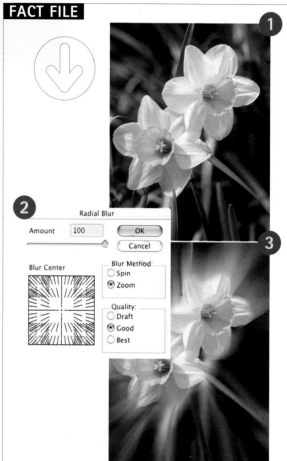

Zoom-burst

The daffodils were perfect for applying a *Radial Blur*. First, I created a duplicate layer. It can be found in the *Blur* filter submenu, in which there is a choice of *Spin* or *Zoom*. *Spin* may be used for creating a shot similar to rotating the camera during exposure, while *Zoom* is very similar to an in-camera zoom-burst technique; using a camera, you zoom the lens from wide to telephoto during a longish exposure. This creates a zoom-burst effect that is emulated by the *Radial Blur* filter. I used the filter at 100% and chose the *Zoom* blur. Finally, I erased the center of the daffodils on the *Zoom* blur layer to let the original distortion-free flowers come through.

Manipulating color, contrast, and tone

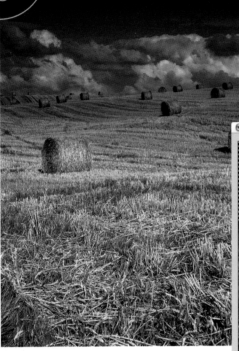

1 This image started off looking slightly gloomy, so the task was to inject some more life and color back in. First of all, I selected the sky so that only its color would be altered.

Most color fixes can be made using adjustment layers, which alter color values without permanantly altering the image. See *Layer > New Adjustment Layer* for the options.

Photoshop Elements has a number of tools at its disposal to allow colors, contrast, and tone to be manipulated in several different ways. By using or combining tools such as the *Levels* command, *Color Variations*, the *Color Cast* quick fix, and the *Hue/Saturation* dialog, you can sort out overarching color problems, brighten or subdue particular colors, desaturate all or part of an image, and fix nearly any contrast or exposure problem you may encounter.

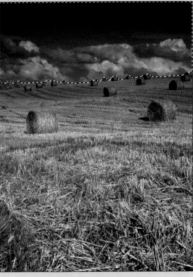

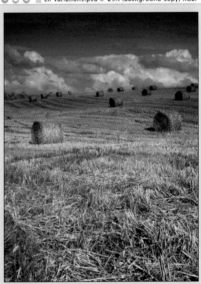

COLOR VARIATIONS

The easiest way to adjust the color of an image is through the *Color Variations* tool (*Enhance > Adjust Colors > Color Variations*). This dialog box has several options available. First, select which area of the image you want to adjust; usually the mid-tones will give the strongest overall color change. Then select the strength of the change using the color-intensity slider. Set it to a subtle level, toward the left-hand side. You can then keep adding color and build up the image slowly, unless you are after a deliberately strong effect—in which case, pull the slider to the right. Use the *Multiple Undo* button to step backward if you take the effect too far. Use the *Reset* button to go back to the beginning.

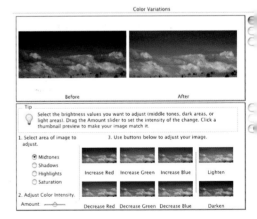

2 I made the sky bluer and lighter, by clicking on *Increase Blue* and then on the *Lighten* button.

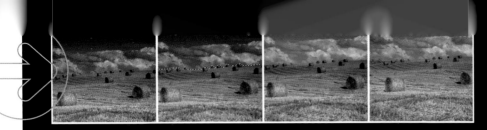

There are a number of different ways of changing color and contrast, depending on the level of correction you want to achieve.

3 I now selected the field, feathering by 35 pixels for a soft transition between the two areas of the image. Without feathering, it would look false, cut-out, and obviously manipulated.

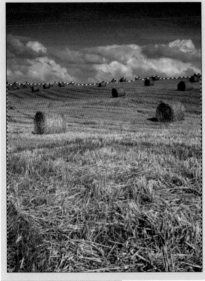

4 Launching *Color Variations* again, I added a small amount of red and yellow to warm the color up. I also moved the intensity slider to the left for a more subtle build-up of color. With the colors in the land and sky beefed up, the final image now has a lot more punch.

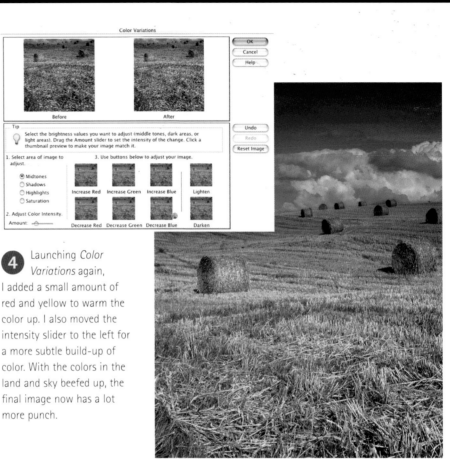

FACT FILE

Enhance	Layer	Select	Filter	V
Quick Fix...				
Auto Levels		⇧⌘L		
Auto Contrast		⌥⇧⌘L		
Auto Color Correction		⇧⌘B		
Adjust Lighting	▸			
Adjust Color	▸	Color Cast...		
Adjust Brightness/Contrast	▸	Hue/Saturation... ⌘U		
		Remove Color ⇧⌘U		
		Replace Color...		
		Color Variations...		

Color cast

The *Color Cast* quick-fix tool (*Enhance > Adjust colors > Color Cast*) should be your first choice if you need to fix an overall color cast. It uses an eyedropper to identify and then neutralize the problem. For the effect to work, you must click on an area that is supposed to be white, neutral gray, or black. This late afternoon shot has turned a little green. I chose the *Color Cast* tool to quickly remove the offending color, having clicked on the white parts of the clouds in the sky to correct the green color cast. It may take several tries to get the color you are after. To avoid creating new color casts, select the problem areas before using the tool.

Manipulating color

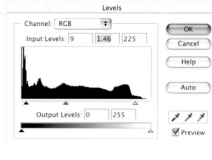

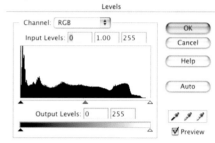

2 Here the histogram suggested that I should move the right-hand slider to the left to brighten the shot. I also moved the gray slider to the left to brighten the midtones of the picture, and finally I moved the black slider a little to the right to increase contrast slightly in the shadows.

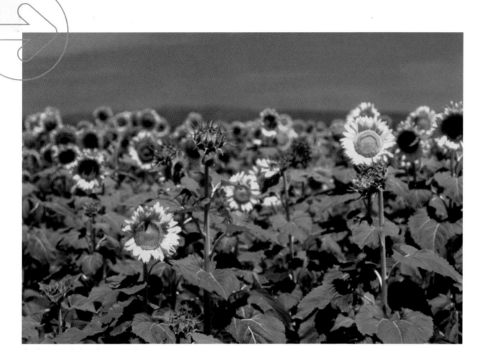

ADJUSTING TONE AND CONTRAST

The *Levels* dialog (*Enhance > Adjust Brightness /Contrast > Levels*) lets you correct color balance and tonal values at the same time. It is the most powerful and precise method of adjusting color and tone.

FIXING CONTRAST/BRIGHTNESS

In the *Levels* dialog, what looks like a mountain range is in fact a histogram of the photograph's pixel tonal range. On the left are the shadows, on the right the highlights, and in between all other tones. Underneath the histogram are three sliders: from left to right, the black slider alters shadows, the gray slider alters midtones, and the white slider alters highlights. To set the black and white points correctly, simply pull the black slider to the right and the white slider to the left so that they meet the first pixels to appear on the mountain range. This will give the optimum tonal and contrast range for the sampled image. You can, of course, adjust these further to make the picture's contrast darker or lighter. For overall changes to the tonal value use the gray slider. Move it to the right for brighter pictures and to the left for darker ones.

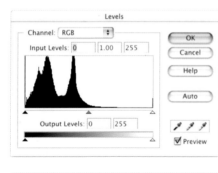

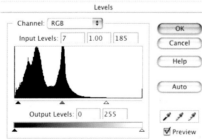

1 The histogram at the top shows that the highlights in this image need brightening. Simply move the white triangle to the right so that it reaches the start of the histogram, as seen in the lower picture.

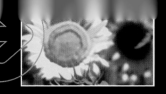
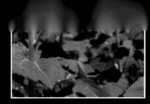

allows the color, contrast and brightness all to be tweaked from one dialog box.

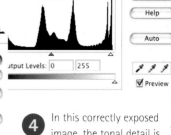

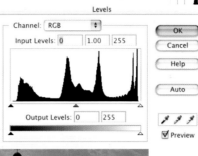

4 In this correctly exposed image, the tonal detail is clearly present on the histogram. The numerous peaks are created by the high-contrast image. By moving the highlight slider from 255 to 247 and the shadow slider from 0 to 11, you create an optimized tonal range showing the maximum amount of detail. You could, of course, tweak the midtone slider to make it darker by moving to the left, or brighter by moving to the right.

FACT FILE

Eyedroppers
You can also use the black and white eyedroppers in the bottom right-hand corner to correct the highlight and shadow points in an image, and adjust the threshold values to pinpoint maximum and minimum values (often called Dmax and Dmin). Hold down the Alt key and drag the white or black slider inward. The posterized threshold image clearly shows where the white and black areas are. Now use the white and black eyedroppers and click in the relevant shadow and highlight areas. This should set the black and white points to give correct tone and color. When using the white eyedropper, do not click on a specular highlight, as this is not a true highlight with detail in it.

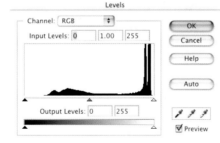

3 In this deliberately overexposed shot you can see that the highlight part of the histogram on the right is peaking out of control, showing that there is a serious loss of highlight detail. The rest of the histogram shows very little detail. This is clearly visible in the original image. The opposite would occur to the left part of the histogram if shadow detail was missing. The normal "mountain range" in the middle is missing, meaning that there is detail not present that cannot be recreated by the computer.

Manipulating color

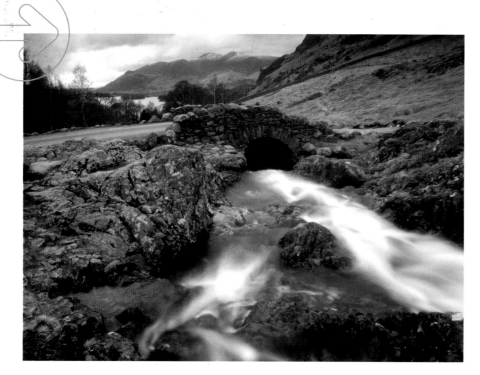

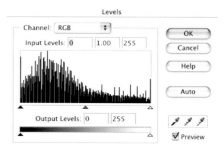

① This example shows exactly what *Levels* can do for your colors. This is the basic shot, without any adjustment to the *Levels*.

TIP Take one image and play around with the slider control in the *Levels* dialog box to get a feel for the way the tool works.

ADVANCED COLOR CONTROLS

While *Levels* is the ideal tool for adjusting the range of tones or the contrast of an image, it's equally capable when it comes to controlling color. In the *Channels* pop-up menu of the *Levels* palette, you can select a single color channel (*Red*, *Blue*, or *Green* in the standard RGB mode) and use the sliders to adjust the color intensity. The gray slider in the *Red* channel turns the picture red when moved to the left and cyan to the right. In the *Green* channel it moves the image toward green when shifted to the left and magenta when moved to the right. The *Blue* channel goes blue to the left and yellow to the right.

Along with the black and white eyedroppers in the bottom right-hand corner, you will find the gray eyedropper, which works in exactly the same way as the *Color Cast* quick-fix tool. Zoom in and try to find a color that should be gray, click on it, and the image should be color-corrected. Sometimes you need to hunt around and try several points before finding a true gray. If you use the black and white eyedroppers to correct highlight and shadow points, you may need the gray eyedropper to fix any color cast that creeps in.

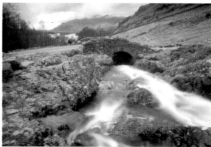

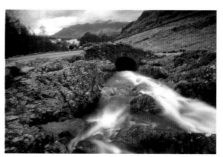

② First of all, I switched to the *Red* color channel and moved the gray slider to the left to accentuate the reds.

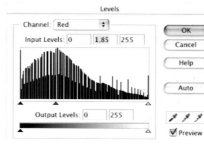

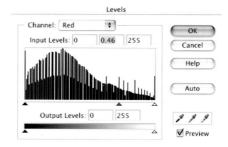

③ This is the same image, with the *Levels* still working on the *Red* channel. This time, by moving the slider to the right I shifted the image toward cyan.

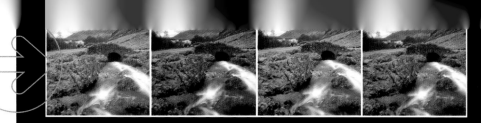

You can create dramatic or subtle color shifts using the *Levels* command. Combine it with selections and adjustment layers for complete control over the colors in your image.

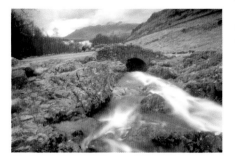

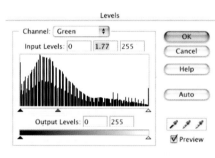

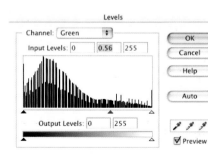

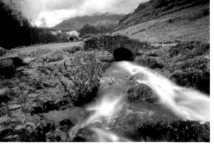

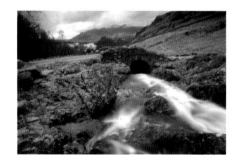

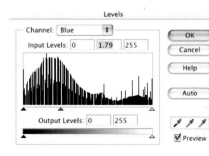

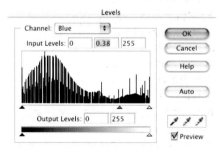

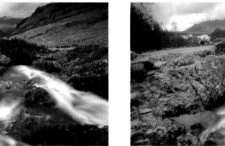

4 I've now switched to the *Green* color channel. This time, moving the slider to the left promotes a green coloring. Moving the slider to the right makes the whole image more magenta.

5 In the *Blue* channel, moving the slider to the left accentuates the blue, while moving it to the right pushes the image toward yellow.

Manipulating color

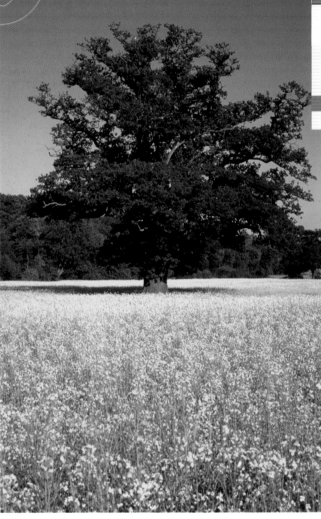

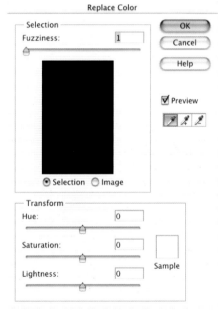

| Enhance | Layer | Select | Filter | Vi |

Quick Fix...
Auto Levels   ⇧⌘L
Auto Contrast   ⌥⇧⌘L
Auto Color Correction   ⇧⌘B

Adjust Lighting   ▶
Adjust Color   ▶   Color Cast...
Adjust Brightness/Contrast   ▶   Hue/Saturation...   ⌘U
                                        Remove Color   ⇧⌘U
                                        Replace Color...
                                        Color Variations...

1 This shot is pretty startling as it is, but we can create some equally impressive effects using the *Replace Color* tool.

2 The *Replace Color* dialog before adjustment. Until you select a color to be adjusted, the sliders won't actually affect any part of your image. You need to click on a color in your photo to activate the controls.

DIGITAL DARKROOM TECHNIQUES

REMOVING AND REPLACING COLORS

Two more tools allow quite radical changes to the coloring of your image. The *Remove Color* tool lets you remove all color from an image and turn it into a black-and-white image. The advantage is that the image isn't converted to grayscale, but remains an RGB image. This is particularly useful if you want to transform a color photo into a black-and-white image without risking its levels of tone or contrast (*see page 102*).

REPLACE COLOR

Enhance > Adjust Color > Replace Color
The second command is a useful tool for both color and black-and-white images that you want to tone with a color. You may, for example, wish to change a specific color in an image without affecting other colors. When the dialog box opens, you click on the color you want to change. Use the + eyedropper to add to the selection. It creates a temporary mask that can be altered with the tolerance slider. You can then use the *Hue* slider to change the selected color. If, for example, the

reds have come out too strong, you can select and alter them. This is very similar to the *Hue/Saturation* tool, with the advantage that you can create your own selection when required. It really comes into its own when coloring black-and-white images.

TIP In images where there is a blue color in the sky and foreground, try selecting the sky first before opening the *Replace Color* dialog box.

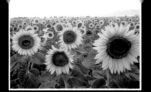
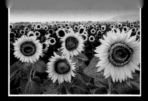
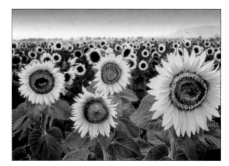

As landscape photographers, we rely on the sun for light. We can use dull conditions to good effect, but some shots demand bright sunlight and clear, blue skies. Luckily, we can always put these in later on in software.

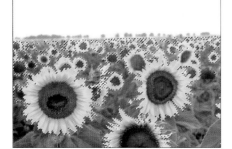

3 In order to enhance the green leaves I chose to select the yellow sunflowers and then invert the selection. With the yellow selected I swapped to the *Lasso* tool and manually selected the centers by hand. Hold down the shift key to add to the selection. Because the sky is pure white, there is no need to select it as its color will not be affected.

Before | After

Tip
💡 Select the brightness values you want to adjust (middle tones, dark areas, or light areas). Drag the Amount slider to set the intensity of the change. Click a thumbnail preview to make your image match it.

1. Select area of image to adjust.
   ○ Midtones
   ○ Shadows
   ○ Highlights
   ○ Saturation
2. Adjust Color Intensity.
   Amount: —○—

3. Use buttons below to adjust your image.
Increase Red | Increase Green | Increase Blue | Lighten
Decrease Red | Decrease Green | Decrease Blue | Darken

4 I now chose *Color Variations* in the *Enhance* menu. The cold leaves need warming up, so I increased green, decreased blue, and increased red. The *Decrease Blue* box increases the yellow by removing blue. Choose the midtone areas for general color changes and a central setting for the *Adjust Color Intensity* slider.

TIP
→ When making tonal changes, try using an adjustment layer. This lets you return at any time and alter your settings; necessary if you change your mind later on in the process.

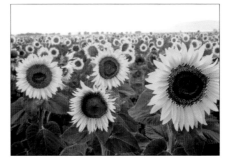

5 I decided to create a sunlike appearance to this shot by highlighting the four dominant sunflowers in the foreground. These will be brightened and the background darkened. First, I selected the middle of the sunflowers and brightened them using *Levels*. I then chose to adjust each flower individually. For a small area such as this it can be easier to use the *Contrast/Brightness* tool instead. Use the *Dodge* and *Burn* tools to manipulate even smaller areas.

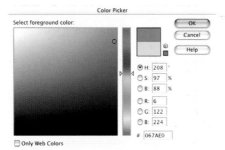

6 The sky now needed some color, so a blue gradation was used. This is similar to using a graduated color filter on your camera lens, but you have much more control over the exact color. The rectangular *Marquee* tool was used and feathered by 15 pixels so that the transition at the bottom wouldn't be hard, jagged, and obvious.

A blue color was chosen from the color picker. Go to the *Set Foreground Color* square on the main menu and double-click it—a dialog box will appear letting you choose a color.

7 The background sunflowers are now selected so that they could be darkened to add to the sun and shadow effect. Carefully go around the edges of the main sunflowers until all the background ones are selected, using the *Lasso* tool. I usually do a rough selection first and then add to it using the Shift key, or delete areas using the Alt key. This lets you quickly build up an accurate selection. After feathering, *Levels* was used to darken the flowers.

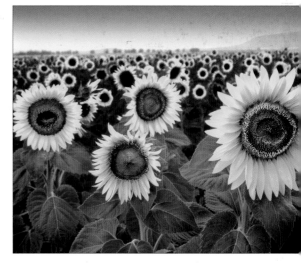

8 The selection was then inverted to brighten the foreground further. When the selection was inverted, I had to deselect the sky area by using the *Lasso* tool while holding down the Alt key. I finally finished off by lightly brushing the leaves with the *Dodge* tool, using a soft brush and an *Exposure* of 10% to add speckled highlights to the leaves.

Rays of light

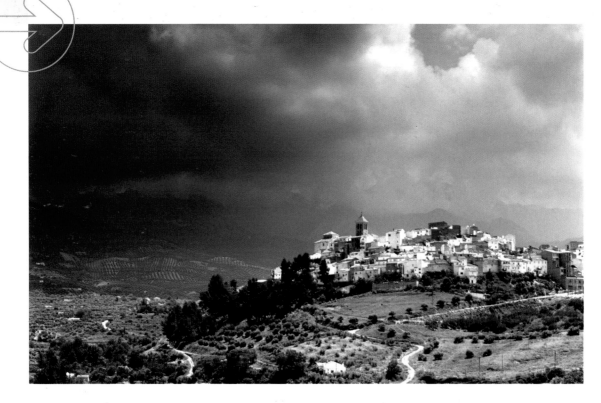

In the original shot I used the shapes of the clouds to create a natural-looking stormy dark cloud, from which the rays of light emerge. Simply select the shape, feather it, and darken it using the Levels dialog box. I then reversed the selection (Select > Inverse) and used the Dodge tool to brighten the other side of the clouds to create a sun-behind-clouds effect.

H ere is another clever trick that adds extra character to a scene. Spectacular storm conditions can be caught on camera, but it takes luck, technique, and patience. When you're running short on one of these, Photoshop Elements can inject some additional drama to the image by adding an artificial lighting effect. While this might seem inappropriate to a "natural" subject like a landscape, the results can be very effective.

 TIP Try looking for a shot that naturally allows for a stormy effect. If you can't find one, then try shooting a stormy sky and dropping it into the scene.

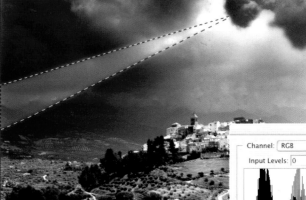

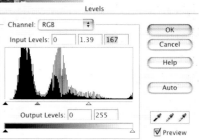

1 Use the *Polygonal Lasso* tool to create a nice straight line. Start the line at a point just inside the stormy cloud from which all the rays emanate, and go to the edge and bring the line back to a small point. It is worth saving each shaft of light as a separate selection so that they can be individually brightened to add a variety of textures to the shot. I feathered the selection by 55 pixels to give a soft edge.

2 With the selection still active, choose *Layer > New Adjustment layer > Levels* and move the midtone slider to the right to create the ray. Using adjustment layers, you can come back and fine-tune the brightness of each ray later to achieve the correct balance.

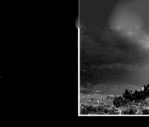
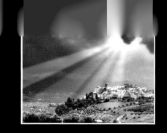

By the careful use of selecting, dull and lifeless shots can be given a new lease of life—some extra va-va-voom!

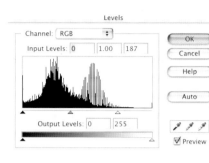

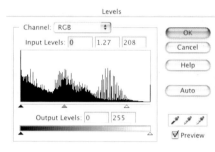

3 Now create more rays of light, using the same technique of soft-edged selections and *Levels* adjustment layers. When you get to the *Levels* palette, use different settings for different rays. This gives the rays different strengths, lending the image a more realistic feeling of depth.

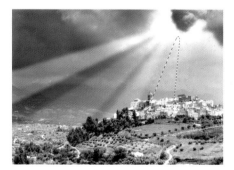

4 Here, I created a shorter ray so I could make the town light up. I also selected the grass just in front of the town, and feathered and brightened it to make it look as if the end of the shaft of light was beginning to spill over. I darkened the foreground to add a sense of depth to the shot. Finally I used the *Burn* tool to darken the natural line of trees.

5 As a finishing touch, I used the *Clone Stamp* to remove one or two intrusive bright houses in the foreground area that had already been darkened.

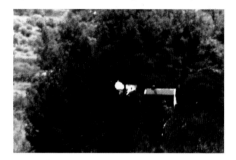

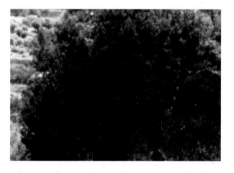

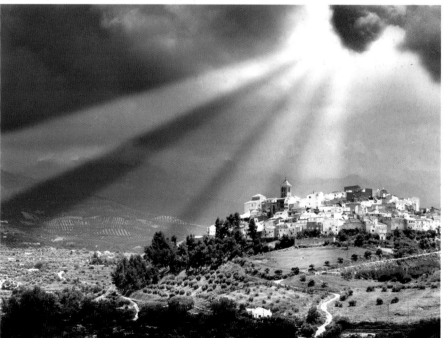

Filters and artistic effects

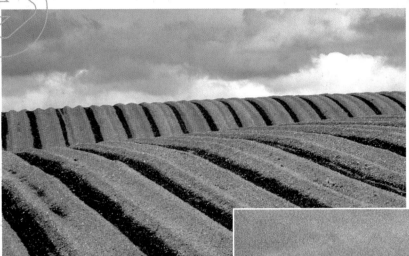

1 There are several types of filters that can produce a grainy effect. Choose strong, bold images with simple detail and texture for this treatment.

2 The *Grain* filter adds random pixels to give the effect of high-speed film. I chose an *Amount* of 60%, *Uniform Distribution* and checked the *Monochromatic* box, which applies the filter using the color present in the image to achieve a purer color.

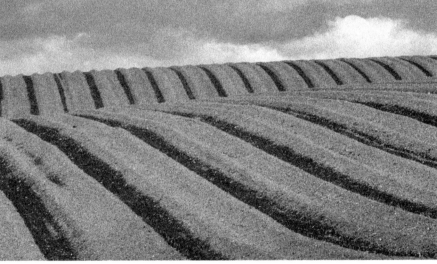

Photoshop Elements comes with a large selection of filters for adding special effects to your images. As with traditional camera filters, it is possible to get carried away with all these effects. Many people think that a filter will rescue a bad photo—it more than likely won't, I'm afraid, but some filters can be used to add interesting effects. Used with care and intelligence, filters can help you produce works of art suitable for framing and hanging.

Try to experiment with different filter mixes and remember that by using the *Opacity* slider, blend modes, and layers, you have a vast combination of different effects available. Third-party companies also produce filter plug-ins, which can be installed into the Photoshop Elements plug-ins folder. Kai's Power Tools from Procreate is a good plug-in to buy once you've become bored with the Adobe filters.

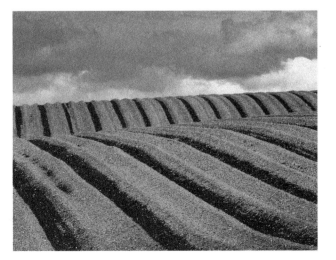

3 It is sometimes better to add extra color saturation and contrast before using the *Grain* filter, as these adjustments are not always so effective when the filter has already been applied.

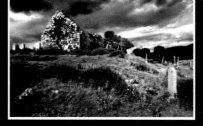

For this variation I used the *Smart Blur* filter, followed by *Underpainting*, followed by *Gaussian Blur*. I placed this layer above the original layer using the *Darken* blend mode.

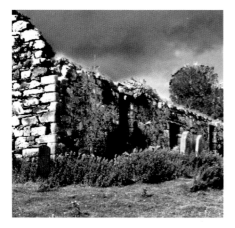

11 I used the *Dodge* tool with a brush size of 75 pixels, selecting the midtones from the range with an *Exposure* of 42%. I then darkened the edges of the wall, which were a little too bright.

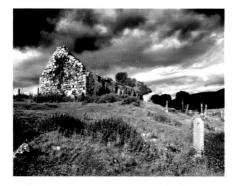

FACT FILE

Adding effects

You can leave the image there, or use some effects filters to get some more intriguing variations.

Copy the layer and apply the filter to the top layer. A traditional darkroom technique is to add a little soft focus to the image during the printing stage. This gives a lovely glow where the shadows bleed into the highlights. Use *Filter > Blur > Gaussian Blur* to create a similar effect in Elements. Create a duplicate layer first and apply the filter effect to this. I chose a strong blur of 50 pixels. This layer was then used with the *Pin Light* blend mode.

I added a further original layer for a new effect. I used the *Find Edges* filter on this and placed the layer at the bottom of the stack. The original layer was placed above it and given a *Linear Light* blend mode.

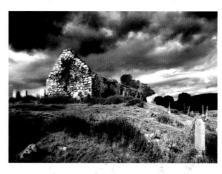

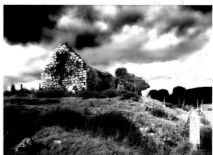

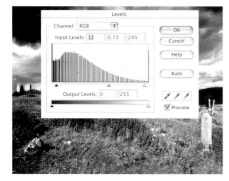

12 Part of the foreground was now selected and feathered. *Levels* was opened once again, and I moved the midtone slider to the right to make the selection darker to complement the rest of the shot.

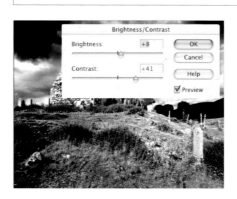

13 Finally, the upper part of the foreground was selected, feathered, and brightened slightly. This time I used the *Brightness/Contrast* tool, nudging the *Brightness* and *Contrast* up to give the effect of sunlight.

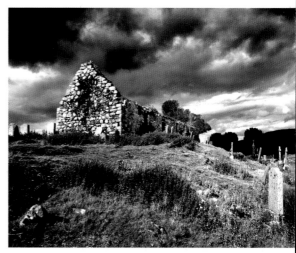

Sepia and duotones

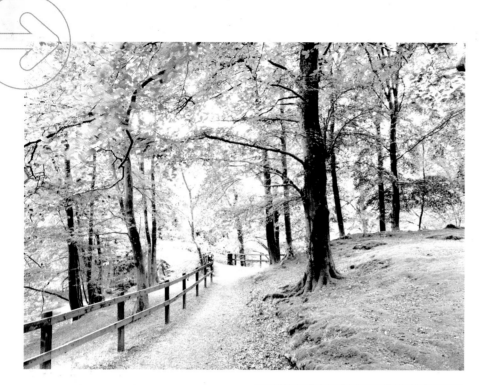

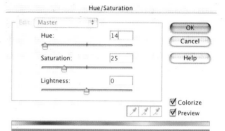

2 Because I was trying to create a sepia color tone, I didn't want to get rid of all of the color in this example. Instead, I chose to tick the *Colorize* button, which automatically creates a color tint to the image. The color of the tint depends on the color you have selected in the *Set Foreground Color* box. Choose a brown for a sepia effect and blue for a blue tint, etc. You can always use the *Hue* slider to try out different color tints. The *Saturation* slider can be used to increase or decrease the color's intensity. The *Lightness* slider, however, should not be altered when creating color tones.

Most images that work in black-and-white will also work well when converted to sepia or another colored tint. Try using the color to add to the mood already present. For example, a winter scene would look odd if it were a warm color, so use the blue end of the spectrum.

The beauty of the computer is that no unpleasant chemicals need to be used to tone the prints, as in traditional photography. For me, the main strength lies in the fine-tuning that is now possible. Precise color shifts can be created with no wasted paper or chemistry. You can also create multicolored tri/quad tones. It has to be said that Adobe Photoshop Elements' big brother, Adobe Photoshop, does offer greater control because it has more tool options to work with, but then it costs a lot more, too.

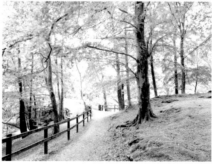

1 The original image can be converted to black and white by choosing to desaturate the colors using *Enhance > Adjust Color > Hue/Saturation*. Push the saturation slider to the far left to remove all color information. If you are starting with a grayscale image, you must convert it to RGB mode, so that color can be added to the image, using *Image > Mode > RGB*.

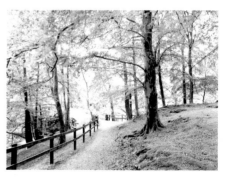

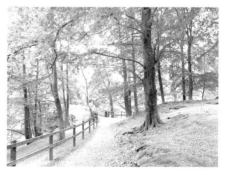

3 The top shot is the effect of using a brown color in the *Set Foreground* color box and selecting *Colorize*. The blue tone is the result of setting a blue color.

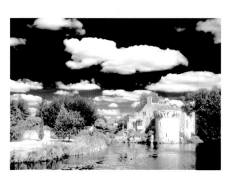

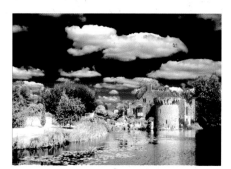

You can achieve an effect similar to color infrared photography by making careful selections with the magic wand tool, then applying excessive *Hue* adjustments using the *Hue/Saturation* control.

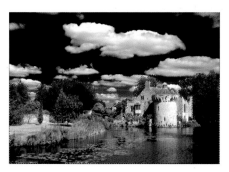

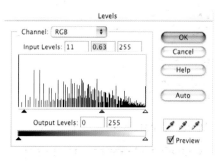

5 Using the original layer again, I created a selection for the foreground, but did not include the castle in the selection because it had lost detail. I feathered the selection by 25 pixels for a soft edge and then chose *Edit> Clear* to remove the dark foreground.

Levels — Channel: Green — Input Levels: 7 1.81 188 — Output Levels: 0 255 — OK Cancel Help Auto — Preview

Levels — Channel: RGB — Input Levels: 11 0.63 255 — Output Levels: 0 255 — OK Cancel Help Auto — Preview

3 Now comes the weird bit. On the new copy layer, I went into *Levels* and chose the *Green* channel. Here I pushed the highlight slider up to 188, the gray slider up to 181 and the black slider to 7. This has brightened and boosted the contrast in the greens. It may look awful, but remember the final image will become black-and-white.

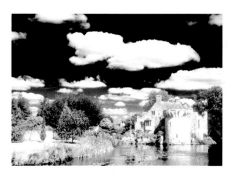

4 I then used the *Enhance > Adjust Color > Remove Color* command to get rid of the now-awful green color. This has given a good infrared-style foliage, but the sky has gone too dark and contrasty.

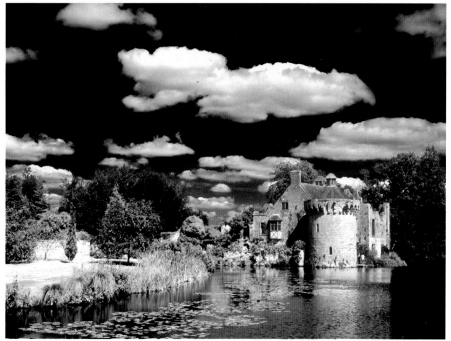

6 This shows the original sky layer combined with the new foreground from the second layer. I thought the foreground was a little too bright, so used the *Levels* command to darken it slightly. The process might seem a little complicated, but you can't deny that it has produced an interesting image.

Making panoramas

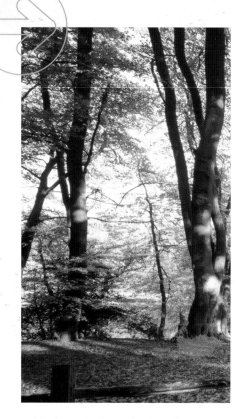

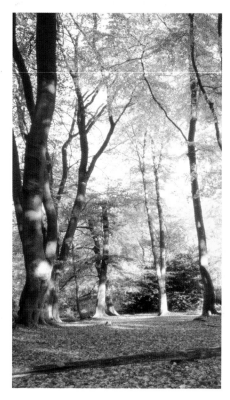

1 The four images I took for this scene were shot with the aid of a tripod and a spirit level. If a job's worth doing, it's worth doing well, and *Photomerge* works better when you put in the groundwork first. I have found that it works best of all if you open each image up on the desktop first. This also lets you check that all the images are present. The software automatically merges any images opened on the desktop when you select *File > Create > Photomerge*.

Adobe Elements has a great feature entitled *Photomerge* that lets you easily create photographic panoramas. To do this, you need to have a selection of shots suitable for making a panorama. Using the wide setting of your lens, take between four and eight portrait shots of your chosen subject. Remember to use the same focal setting for each shot, as changing the setting by zooming in will ruin the effect, and try to shoot from the same position. Using the same exposure for each shot helps to maintain consistency.

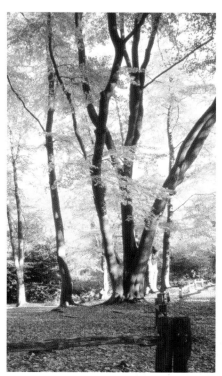

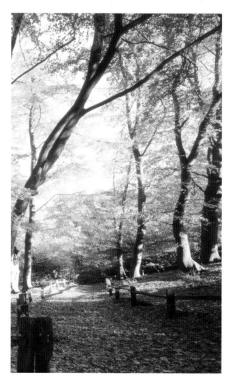

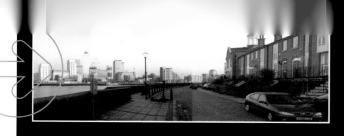

A tripod and spirit level will make taking shots for panoramas much easier. Obviously, the tripod keeps the shots nice and straight and allows more precise alignments than handholding the camera. The spirit level should be used before each shot to keep the camera angle consistent as you rotate the viewpoint.

You can shoot more frames if you want a wrap-around effect, and you can also use the landscape format if you wish. However, the process tends to chop off top and bottom, meaning that too much image may be lost. Landscapes also suffer more from wide-angle distortion, so the merged shots may look a little strange.

The main trick is to make sure each picture overlaps the next by about 20%. This allows the software plenty of scope to produce a nice, soft, seamless transition from one shot to the next. Too much or not enough overlap can cause problems. This technique works well with any subject, whether landscape, cityscape, or even an interior.

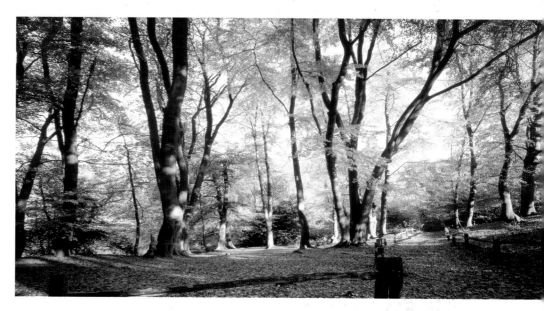

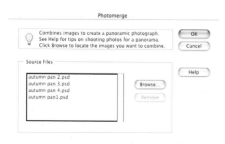

2 The *Browse* dialog box opens to confirm your selection. Choose the *Browse* option to add further images or to choose an entirely different set from scratch.

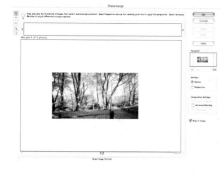

3 Click *OK* and the *Photomerge* software automatically merges the selected images to create a panorama.

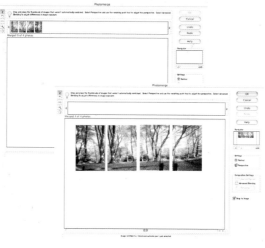

4 At times *Photomerge* needs a little help, and the whole process becomes much harder. You may have to manually drag each image from the light box to the work area yourself, using the *Move* tool. You then have to judge by eye where each image overlaps. This is a lot more difficult than you might imagine, as what looks like a good overlap can end up with gaps in it after processing. Try clicking the *Snap To Image* box, as this helps the software to detect a good match when manually merging two or more images.

5 This is the final result. In some cases, you may find some areas of sky have irregular color and density. Checking the *Advanced Blending* mode should minimize any exposure differences between shots, but does not always work. If not, I generally use the *Gradation* tool to put a color grad over the problem.

A successful *Photomerge* should have little distortion to the images at the edges. Don't use a really wide wide-angle lens or the resulting distortion will not be easily rectifiable.

TIP There is a special panorama head available for tripods. This allows the process to be done very accurately, for truly professional results.

Montage: windmill at sunset

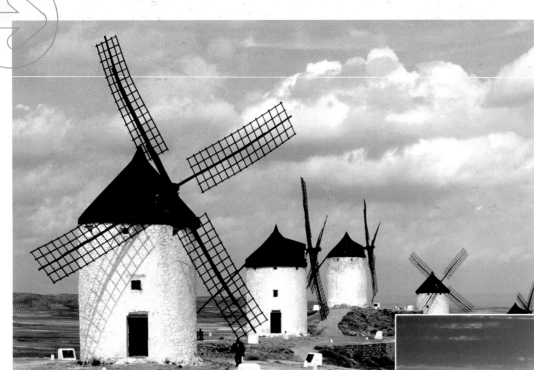

1 The original was quite a nice shot taken during the day, but due to nagging family members I couldn't hang about for the shot I really wanted—a sunset. I decided instead to create my own sunset. I quickly realized that the key to this would be a selection mask for the windmills.

By now it should be clear that the natural approach to landscape isn't always the most effective, and by making larger changes to the colors or tones, or even introducing new elements into the frame, you can create really exciting images. Now we're going to take this concept one step farther, showing how you can composite multiple images to create a vista that looks as natural or unnatural as you want, but which has never actually existed.

2 The original shot was taken with a moderate telephoto lens. I needed to find a suitable sea sunset. The windmills would go black, simulating a silhouette, so I wanted a strong yet simple sunset that was not too dark or the windmills would get lost in the background.

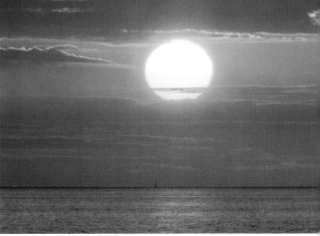

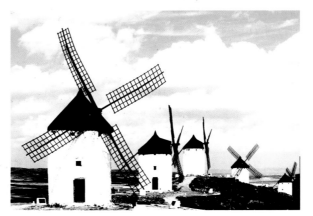

3 First I created a selection mask to turn the white windmills black, by creating a high-contrast image first. Create a new copy layer of the background. Choose *Brightness/Contrast* and boost both. This allows much sharper transitions in color and density, which in turn allow for easier selections.

Understanding the difference between screen resolution and printed resolution is the key to getting perfect prints from your digital images.

WHAT RESOLUTION OR DPI/PPI DO YOU ACTUALLY NEED TO PRINT AT?

Basically this boils down to how the eye perceives detail. The human eye can only resolve detail up to certain limits. For most printed purposes, where the image is viewed at 8–12 inches, this equates to an image of 300 to 400dpi/ppi. Such a resolution is ideal for our brain to be able to visualize the image as a continuous tone.

INK AND PAPER

Until you have enough confidence to choose inks from other suppliers, I would advise using the manufacturer's inks. Some companies such as Lyson produce high-quality inks that rival manufacturers' own inks, but in general it is advisable to use only Epson or Canon inks in their respective printers. Beware cheap inks! They often clog up the nozzles and produce inferior print quality. In the long run they cost more because they are so unreliable.

Papers, on the other hand, offer much more choice. I rarely use manufacturers' own-brand paper and prefer ICI Olmec paper. I use a glossy heavyweight 260g paper, which yields good blacks and good colors. It prints extremely well on Epson and Canon printers. Matte photo papers are also good and may be perfect for framing as there is less glare from reflections compared to glossy prints. There are many other brands out there that offer a good compromise between price and quality. You may like to try out several brands to find the one that suits you. Papers don't cause problems with printers in most cases, but take care if using non-inkjet papers and do careful tests first as these could jam inside the printer.

Different papers will give surprisingly different results from the same file printed on the same printer. I suggest sticking to one brand to maintain consistency in printing, though it is possible to create and save custom color print profiles using the printer software.

You can then simply choose the profile from the *Custom* menu bar. One paper, for example, may print with too much magenta, so you can dial in less magenta and save the profile instead of manually correcting the color.

CHOOSING THE RIGHT PRINTER

If your ultimate goal is to produce top-quality landscape prints, you will need a good printer or all your hard work will be for nothing. Look out for a printer that offers photorealistic printing and check print samples carefully. Try to get a printer with at least six color inks. The extra light cyan/magenta inks make much smoother tones in the print quality. You can also get printers with light black ink for even greater tonal control. Make sure you buy a printer with separate ink cartridges for each color (i.e., six or seven separate ink cartridges). All-in-one ink cartridges waste huge amounts of ink. When one color has finished, all the others have to be thrown away.

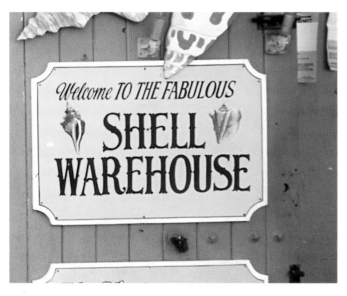

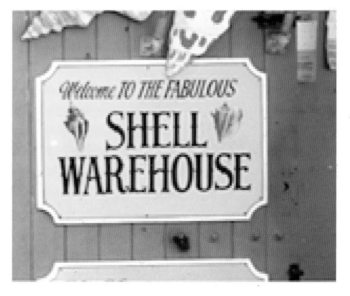

At 300ppi there are enough pixels to produce photo-quality output. Pushing the image resolution past this point will rarely have any benefit when the shot is printed out.

The screen is far more forgiving when it comes to image resolution. If viewed at actual size; a 72ppi image will appear to be photo quality. It is only when the image is printed out that the pixels that make up the shot become obvious. For Web or e-mail use, 72ppi is perfectly adequate.

Perfect prints

Image Size

Pixel Dimensions: 17.2M

Width: 2835 pixels
Height: 2126 pixels

[OK] [Cancel] [Auto...]

Document Size:

Width: 240.03 mm
Height: 180 mm
Resolution: 300 pixels/inch

☑ Constrain Proportions
☑ Resample Image: Bicubic

1 Picture quality depends on the resolution of your image. Try to use 300dpi as your standard document resolution. You also need to make the photo the correct size for the paper. If you have enough resolution for a US-letter sized print, make sure there is room for a small border around the edge of the paper.

Page Setup

Settings: Page Attributes
Format for: Stylus Photo 830
EPSON Stylus Photo 830
Paper Size: A4
20.99 cm x 29.69 cm
Orientation: [landscape] [portrait] [landscape]
Scale: 100 %

[?] [Cancel] [OK]

2 Choose *File* > *Page Setup* from the main *Menu Bar*. Select landscape or portrait orientation and your chosen print size. You can also choose scale or borderless printing on newer printers.

TIP Try to print during the day so that you can use window light to check the colors are true to life. Looking at a print under artificial tungsten lights will make it appear warmer than it is. Under fluorescent or low-energy bulbs it may even look green.

Print

Printer: Stylus Photo 830
Presets: Standard
Print Settings
Media Type: Plain Paper
Ink: ◉ Color ○ Black
Mode: ◉ Automatic Quality ——— Speed
○ Custom
○ Advanced Settings
Print Quality: Photo
☑ MicroWeave
☑ High Speed
☐ Flip Horizontal
☐ Finest Detail

[Help]

[?] [Preview] [Save As PDF...] [Cancel] [Print]

3 Choose *File* > *Print Preview*. This is useful, as you will automatically see if you've chosen the wrong orientation—this can save wasted paper and ink in the long run.

Print

Printer: Stylus Photo 830
Presets: Best colour print
Print Settings
Media Type: Premium Glossy Photo Paper
Ink: ◉ Color ○ Black
Mode: ○ Automatic
○ Custom
◉ Advanced Settings
Print Quality: Best Photo
☑ MicroWeave
☑ High Speed
☐ Flip Horizontal
☑ Finest Detail

[Help]

[?] [Preview] [Save As PDF...] [Cancel] [Print]

4 Now would be a good time to put some paper in the printer! Remember to put the paper in the right way up. Gloss is easy, but some single-sided matte papers are difficult to judge, especially in artificial light at night. The whiter side is the one to print on. Mark the envelope or packaging so you know which is the front, for future printing.

Print

Printer: Stylus Photo 830
Presets: Best colour print
Color Management
◉ Color Controls Gamma: 1.8
○ ColorSync
○ No Color Adjustment
Mode: Vivid
Brightness 0
Contrast 0
Saturation 4
Cyan ○ 6
Magenta ● -4
Yellow ○ 5

[Help]

[?] [Preview] [Save As PDF...] [Cancel] [Print]

5 When you are happy with the size and layout, select *File* > *Print*. Before you press the button, it is well worth doing a final check on the most important settings.

Print

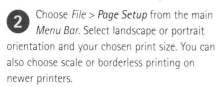

Position
Top: mm
Left: mm
☑ Center Image

Scaled Print Size
Scale: 100% ☐ Scale to Fit Media
Height: 179.917 mm
Width: 239.889 mm
☑ Show Bounding Box
☐ Print Selected Area

☑ Show More Options

Output
[Background...] [Screen...] ☐ Calibration Bars ☐ Caption
[Border...] [Transfer...] ☐ Registration Marks ☐ Labels
[Bleed...] ☐ Interpolation ☐ Corner Crop Marks ☐ Emulsion Down
☐ Center Crop Marks ☐ Negative

☐ Include Vector Data
Encoding: Binary

6 The printer dialog box will open. You can use the basic auto-print, photo enhance, or custom. Choose a paper type: if you don't have an exact match, use the closest one on the list. Use *Speed* for quick, unimportant work and *Quality* for best work. Click on *Custom* and then *Advanced* to create your own profiles. Use the color controls in the *Color Management* section and play around with the settings until you get a perfect print. This may take a while! You can then save the setting for future use. Finally, hit the *Print* button.

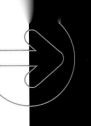
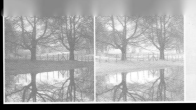
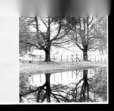

In Photoshop proper, standard RGB (Red, Green, Blue) images should be converted to CMYK (Cyan, Magenta, Yellow, Black) prior to printing. Elements takes care of this for you automatically.

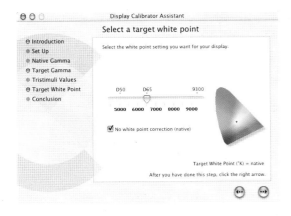

Callibrating your display is a chore, but one that makes a difference when it comes to printing and sharing your shots. You need accurate color across every device in the chain to get superb prints.

1 Choose *Custom* in your printer dialog box. Then choose advanced.

2 Choose *Color Controls* in *Color Management.*

3 You now need to decide if the print is too dark or too light, and what color to add or subtract. Density, contrast, and saturation are straightforward. Working out a color cast is not always easy, but trial and error should get you there in the end. For quality results, uncheck *High Speed* and check *Finest Detail.* Choose a paper and print quality setting for the job in hand.

4 Once happy with the color and density, you can save the setting. Do as many tests as you like for different papers.

POOR COLOR QUALITY

Bad color casts or the wrong density can be a problem. If they are, then you will have to calibrate your monitor or your printer. This simply means matching up the print to the monitor, or vice versa, for reliable printouts. Your monitor may be too dark or too green, for example, so any color corrections you do will be wrong in the first place. You have two options. Firstly, use a custom printer profile to correct the problem at the print stage; or, secondly, calibrate your monitor. Often you may need to do both. Calibrate the monitor and then the printer.

MONITOR CALIBRATION

The monitor can give inaccurate colors and density. The room lighting can also affect the monitor's colors, so I advise you to use a black-card cover 6-8 inches around the monitor to stop reflections. This is easy to make and need not be attached permanently. Don't let strong sunlight reflect off the monitor and cause glare.

You can use Adobe Gamma correction supplied with Adobe Photoshop Elements. It may already be installed on your computer, so check your control panels first. The calibration process is fairly straightforward, but you can use a wizard if necessary. A tip is to squint when trying to fade the gray boxes together—it's much easier. You should also try to do it in a darkened room for greater accuracy.

PRINT CALIBRATION

The following example is for an Epson printer, but Canon and other manufacturers' printer calibration methods will follow a similar process.

FACT FILE

TIP Reducing colors in the printer color correction will use less ink than increasing a color.

Understanding color corrections

Print is	Color variations in Elements	Printer color correction
TOO CYAN	Increase red	Reduce cyan or increase magenta + yellow
TOO YELLOW	Increase blue	Reduce yellow or increase cyan + magenta
TOO MAGENTA	Increase green	Reduce magenta or increase cyan + yellow
TOO GREEN	Increase magenta	Increase magenta or reduce cyan + yellow
TOO BLUE	Increase yellow	Increase yellow or reduce cyan + magenta
TOO RED	Increase cyan	Increase cyan or reduce magenta + yellow

Creative borders

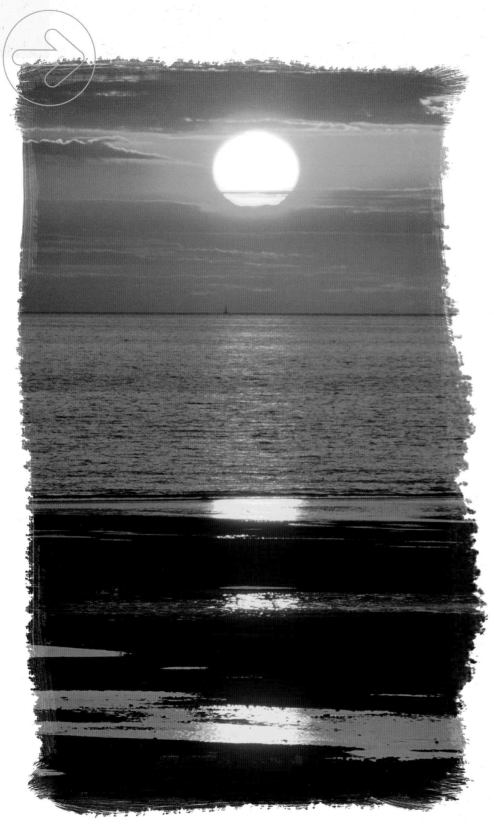

Adding a border around your image helps to provide the finishing touch to your work. Although Adobe Photoshop Elements has several borders and frames to choose from in the *Effects > Frames* menu, they will soon become monotonous to use.

1 For this shot, I used a pre-drawn black mask made using black ink on paper. The image was scanned in using a flatbed scanner and imported into the sunset shot. With the black mask on a separate layer, choose *Screen* from the blending mode pull-down list. The blending modes are very powerful and can produce really cool effects.

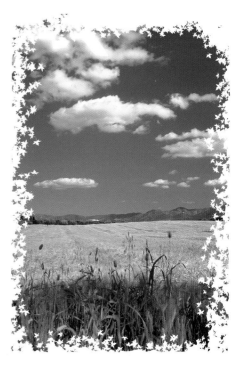

2 I used the *Eraser* tool and the *Maple Leaf* brush to create this interesting border design. Keep altering the brush size for varied leaf sizes.

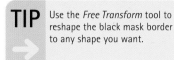

Photoshop Elements offers a number of border effects in the *Effects > Frames* menu. Some are useful and some are a little over the top. The *Layer Styles* palette is another great source of creative border effects.

Why not try to make your own border? It isn't that hard and you will be the proud owner of your own unique border style.

Although you can buy some great plug-in filters for borders from companies like Extensis, it is more fun and more rewarding to create your own, not to mention a lot cheaper! There are several different ways to make them.

TIP Hundreds of everyday objects can be employed as frames if you scan them. Try using a black cloth over any 3D objects you scan to stop stray light and flare wrecking the shot.

TIP Use the *Free Transform* tool to reshape the black mask border to any shape you want.

FLATBED SCANNING

If you have a flatbed scanner, you can draw your own border on paper. This opens up many different permutations of paper and media that you can use. Try watercolor paper and wet paints and scan the results in. You could even scan a real picture frame or any other 3D object using a flatbed scanner. The only limits are your imagination!

CAMERA COPY

You can also use a camera to copy the artwork and input this file onto your computer.

BRUSHED BORDERS

This is perhaps the easiest route to take. Start by creating a new layer, filling it with white and placing it underneath the image. Now resize the canvas so that it is several inches larger all around. You can now use the Impressionist brush (click and hold on the *Brush* icon in the *toolbar*) to paint a border underneath or on the actual image. You can also use the eraser brush to remove image information rather than adding to it with the paint brush.

TIP To fill a layer with solid color, double-click the *Set Foreground Color* box in the *Toolbar*. Choose a color from the *Color Picker*, then choose *Edit > Fill* and click *OK*.

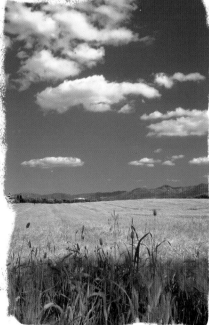

3 A simpler brush design, produced by a soft brush being used to remove parts of the image for a subtle, "sponged" effect.

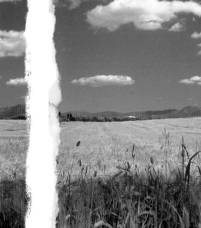

4 I ended up erasing the entire border three times—the *Opacity* was gradually increased each time I had finished going round.

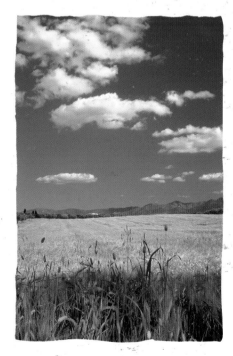

5 A simpler and cleaner edge effect created by going around once at maximum 100% *Opacity*.

Greetings card

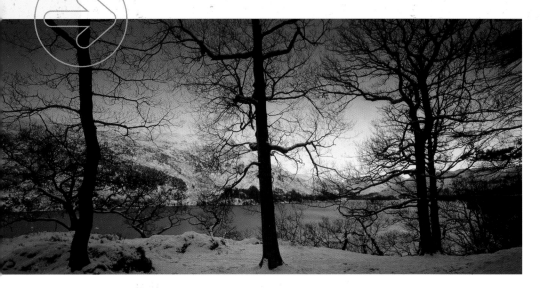

3 The background color of the card will be a blue color to echo the cool colors of winter in the original. With the original winter image still open on the screen, I used the *Eyedropper* tool to select a blue to maintain a link between the photograph and the background colors. The blue color should now appear in the *Set Foreground Color* square on the left-hand-side tool menu. I then clicked back onto the new page and then chose *Edit > Fill* to apply the color to the entire page. This will now become your background page with the photo in a layer on top of it.

Creating a greetings card will give your work a professional and slick appearance. You can use these cards to impress your friends—or even to send to an important client, who might be flattered by a bespoke and unusual gift. Once you have made the design template, you can reuse it time after time.

1 The first thing you need to do is find a suitable photograph that reflects what you are trying to portray. Here, I've chosen a moody winter shot. You will need to keep the original photo open and create a new document for the card itself.

New

Name: greeting card	OK
Image Size: 25M	Cancel
Preset Sizes: Custom	
Width: 8.3 inches	
Height: 11.7 inches	
Resolution: 300 pixels/inch	
Mode: RGB Color	

Contents
- White
- Background Color
- Transparent

2 The next hurdle is to decide what size you want the card to be. Here I've chosen a panoramic format, so the card's dimensions will have to fit the photo. I've decided that I will print onto a sheet of paper measuring 8.3 x 11.7 inches. Use the *Image Size* dialog box to create this size. Choose white as the background color and a resolution of 300ppi to maintain good-quality printing. You are now ready to fill the card with your background color, which should be sympathetic to your photo.

Fill

Contents
Use: Foreground Color

OK
Cancel
Help

Custom Pattern:

Blending
Mode: Normal
Opacity: 100 %
Preserve Transparency

greeting card @ 16.7% (RGB)

16.67%   8.3 inches x 11.7 inches

TIP In many instances you can resize the image before pasting it into a new document, then make any minor changes of scale using the *Transform > Scale* tool.

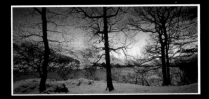

Creating your own greetings cards is a simple and easy way to show off your work to friends and family.

4 It is now time to paste the winter image into the new A4 page that has been created. Check that the image resolution is the same for the photo and the document. If not, use the *Image > Resize > Image Size* to correct the resolution. Select all and use the *Move* tool to manually drag the image across to the card page. It's easier if you have both windows open and next to each other when performing this. In this case, the photo was much larger than the page was—don't panic! Use *Edit > Transform > Scale* to resize the image. Simply drag the corner handlebar with the mouse. To maintain a proportional size, hold down the shift key while resizing. Alternatively, use the percentage values in the *Menu Bar* at the top. Click the middle icon and fill in a percentage in one of the boxes. Make sure there is a border of equal width on both sides and on the bottom. If necessary, select the *Move* tool and use the arrows on the keyboard for very precise incremental movements.

5 For a more professional look, a thin white border was added around the image. Use *Select > All* and then *Edit > Stroke* and a dialog box will appear. Enter 3 in the *Width* box for a 3-pixel-wide border. Next, double-click the color box to make the color picker appear and choose a suitable color, in this case white. Click *OK* and a white border will appear around the image. You could at this stage add a bevel edge or other effect from the *Layer Style* menu.

6 Next, some type was added to the image. The *Type* tool is a very powerful vector tool within the Adobe Photoshop Elements software that allows for the creation of some sophisticated styles. Because of this you don't need to buy an expensive page-layout package.

For the font I chose Papyrus Regular with a size of 45. Before typing, select a color from the color picker in the *Options Bar*, or double-click the *Set Foreground Color* icon. You can change the color at any time by selecting the type first. Click on the *Type* tool and a new layer is automatically created—simply click in the area where you wish to begin writing. If the size is too big or too small, you can create a new font size by selecting the type with your mouse and typing in a new number. If you are familiar with typing in a word-editing package, these skills will come in handy when using the *Type* tool.

By floating the mouse cursor just to the side of the type, the icon changes to a *Move* tool, letting you move the type manually by dragging it.

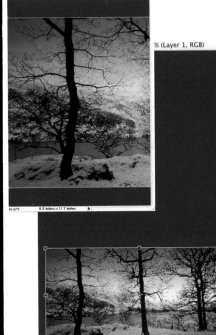

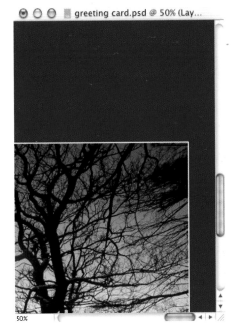

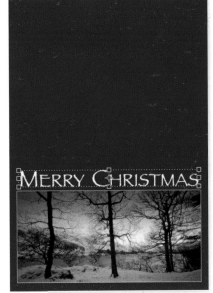

Greetings card

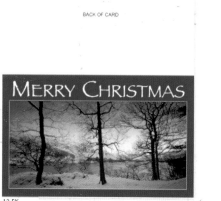

greeting card.psd @ 12.5% (B...

BACK OF CARD

MERRY CHRISTMAS

12.5%

greeting cardfront.psd @ 15% (solid colour, RGB)

BACK OF CARD

MERRY CHRISTMAS

14.96%   8.3 inches × 11.7 inches

8 The card was now a different size from the paper. This meant I had to crop it, so that an exact-sized copy could be made to allow the inside text to be designed and placed accurately within a template. To find out the exact size of the bottom half, I created a new layer and then selected the bottom half of the card, again with the *Rectangular Marquee*, filling it with a different solid color (green) while still on a new layer. This was then moved up until the two halves were back to back, clearly showing me where to crop the remaining white so that two equal halves were made for folding later. You can design the image to fit any shape. Keeping the two halves equal at the start will make this project easier.

7 To save on ink, the back of the card was made white. I created a new layer and selected the area above the red line with the *Rectangular Marquee* tool. I chose a white color, then used *Edit > Fill* to turn it white. This layer was placed above the blue background layer.

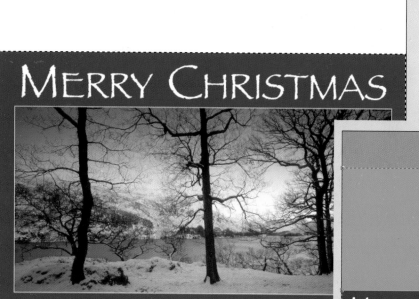

greeting cardfront.psd @ 25% (red line, RGB)

MERRY CHRISTMAS

25%   8.3 inches × 11.7 inches

9 I used the *Crop* tool to remove the surplus white area at the top, using the green template as a guide. I then turned off the solid color layers visibility as it was no longer needed.

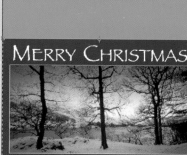

BACK OF CARD

MERRY CHRISTMAS

SHOWING YOUR PICTURES

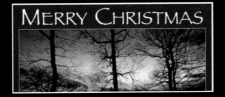

You can use the basic ideas and techniques in this step-by-step project to create other designs, such as a photographic letterhead for your stationery.

10 I opened the image size to make a note of the size and resolution, then created a new document using the same size and resolution. By keeping both documents open, I was able to select the solid green color layer and drag it to the new document. This recreated the green template so that text could be correctly designed and accurately placed.

New

Name:	inside card	OK
ge Size: 21.7M		Cancel
t Sizes:	Custom	
	Width: 8.3	inches
	Height: 10.163	inches
	Resolution: 300	pixels/inch
Mode:	RGB Color	

tents
ite
kground Color
nsparent

11 Next, create a new layer for the design located at the bottom of the card. Make a selection using the *Rectangular Marquee* tool to create a rectangle. Choose *Edit > Stroke* to create a blue border effect. I used a *Width* of 20 pixels and checked the *Inside* button in the *Location* box. The color selected was blue, in keeping with the winter effect.

Stroke

Stroke		OK
Width:	20 px	Cancel
Color:		Help

Location
◉ Inside ○ Center ○ Outside

Blending
Mode: Normal
Opacity: 100 %
☐ Preserve Transparency

Spatter

	OK
	Cancel

200%

Spray Radius	20
Smoothness	2

12 Finally, the *Spatter* filter was used to add texture. This is located in the *Brush Strokes* section. I chose a *Spray Radius* of 20 and a *Smoothness* of 2 for a coarse result.

FACT FILE

For a different look
Add a little fun to the text box by using the *Liquify* filter to distort the shape of the box. For the "one whiskey too many" look you can distort the text as well, using the *Warp* tool!

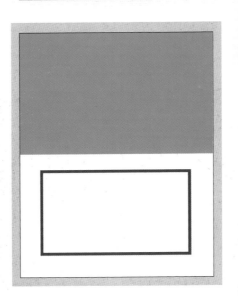

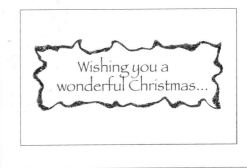

TIP Try a mock-up card using a sheet of paper similar to the one you are going to print on and roughly draw how you want the design to look. This is a useful reference guide.

Calendar

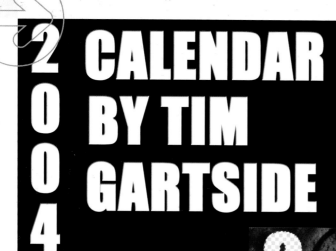

1 I used a bold typeface, "Impact," to let me make the text transparent later on, so that images would show through. Each line was created on a separate layer so that they could be moved independently. The 200pt font size was set manually to make the text fit the page, and I also used *Layer Styles* to create a bevel, adding shape and form to the text.

2 I used a photograph of some frozen glass beads as an alternative to the black background. Simply select the type, then go back to the blue bead layer and clear to reveal the photographs underneath. Use the *Layer Styles* to create the bevel effect again.

Some projects need to be split into manageable parts. I created this calendar in two sections—a front cover and an inside-page template. Both documents have been created to print out on a single sheet of paper, with a width of 11.7 inches and a height of 8.3 inches. The resolution is 300 ppi.

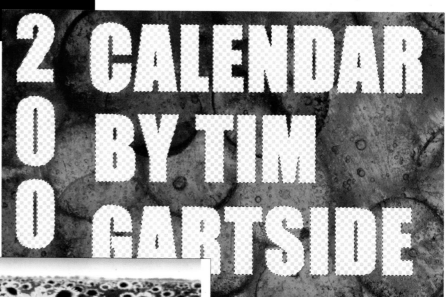

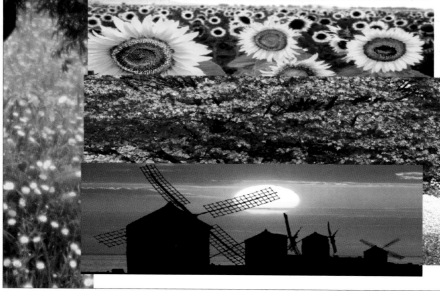

3 Several photographs were opened and imported to the front-cover document, before resizing with the *Free Transform* tool. For this you should select pictures that are bright and vibrant or they may make the typeface difficult to read.

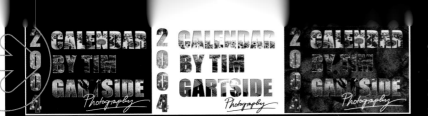

If you are intending to print many copies, then choose the background color with care, as black or any other solid color will use up a huge amount of ink. Use double-sided glossy or mat paper, and print one month on each side so that you only use half the paper.

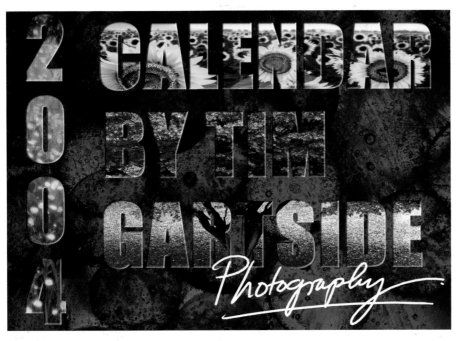

4 Finally, as a finishing touch I used a Wacom Art Pad to write the word "Photography," which I placed in its own layer before resizing.

That's the outside taken care of. It's time to move on to the inside calendar page.

FACT FILE

Typeface heading
This group of typefaces shows how different *Layer Effects* can radically transform an ordinary black-on-white typeface.

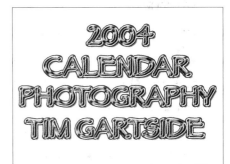

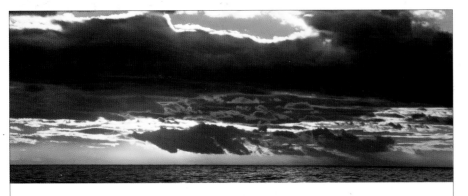

5 This is the basic design for the calendar-page template. I have split the page into an area for dates and an image. I will create two documents for the image and the dates and merge them together later.

Calendar

CREATING THE TEMPLATE DOCUMENT

Creating the grid and dates is a slow process, but one that is necessary for a professional look. You should be able to save the grid and text on separate layers so that amendments can be made for each month. This will be your master template, which you can duplicate for each month. Remember you can also make the calendar smaller by resizing it at the final stage. Use the *Save As* command to give it a new name. Remember to choose photos that reflect the particular month of the year.

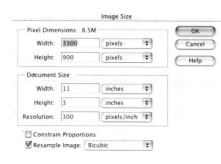

1 A separate document for the date template was created measuring 11 x 3 inches and 300dpi/ppi.

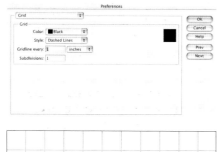

2 I used the grid so that aligning the dates would be easier. In *Edit > Preferences > Grid*, create a gridline every 1 inch. This creates a grid that is 11 squares long by three columns high.

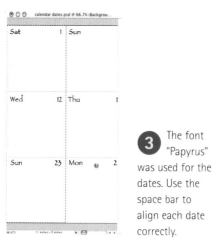

3 The font "Papyrus" was used for the dates. Use the space bar to align each date correctly.

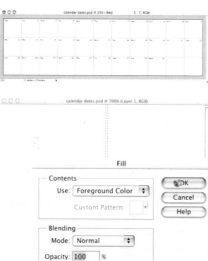

4 Create a new layer so that the box outline can be constructed. Use the *Rectangular Marquee* tool to create a line from top to bottom. Make it as thin as possible by zooming in to 700%, and then fill the line with black. Copy this layer and move it along to the next vertical grid line, then repeat the process and merge the thin line layers together.

TIP To cut down on printing costs consider sending a PDF or JPEG, if the recipient has a computer, or alternatively design using a smaller page size.

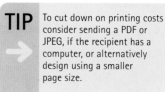

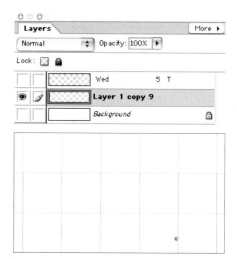

5 Repeat the process to produce the horizontal lines, then flatten all the layers and import to the calendar-page template document.

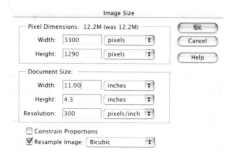

6 The final page document needs to be a width of 11 inches by a height of 4.3 inches with a resolution of 300ppi. It should produce a nice panoramic effect in the final calendar design. A photograph of a sunset was opened and pasted into the photo template. It was then moved up and down until I was happy with the composition.

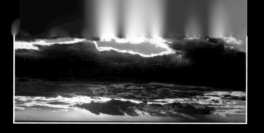

Creating a calendar is a big project but the end result has a powerful visual impact. Calendars can be a great way to present your work to others, or even sell your photography to potential clients.

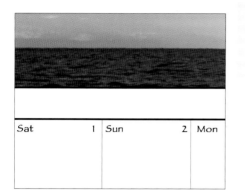

Sat	1	Sun	2	Mon

7 The layers were then flattened and the image exported to the calendar-page template. With the photo and date as two separate layers above the white background layer, I now moved the two layers to create the final design.

FACT FILE

Binding
To complete this project, you will have to create 12 pages and a front cover and then have the whole lot bound! It may be worth buying a spiral binder for this, or you could go to a main-street print store and have them do the job for you.

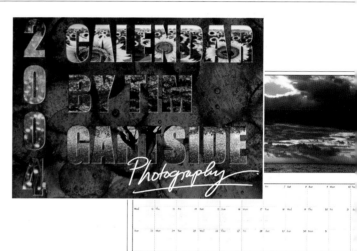

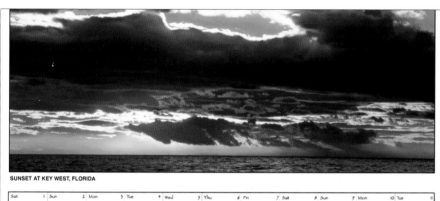

SUNSET AT KEY WEST, FLORIDA

Sat	1	Sun	2	Mon	3	Tue	4	Wed	5	Thu	6	Fri	7	Sat	8	Sun	9	Mon	10	Tue	11
Wed	12	Thu	13	Fri	14	Sat	15	Sun	16	Mon	17	Tue	18	Wed	19	Thu	20	Fri	21	Sat	22
Sun	23	Mon	24	Tue	25	Wed	26	Thu	27	Fri	28	Sat	29	Sun	30	Mon	31				

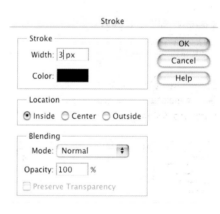

Stroke

Stroke
Width: 3 px
Color: ▮

OK
Cancel
Help

Location
⦿ Inside ◯ Center ◯ Outside

Blending
Mode: Normal
Opacity: 100 %
☐ Preserve Transparency

9 For an extra touch I created a *Stroke* line around each box, with a stroke *Width* of 3 to 6 pixels and a black color.

8 I used the *Type* tool to add a subtitle in Helvetica Bold, 10pt and then created a new layer for the month. I chose a pale gray color and a 200pt font size and wrote across the dates. I then adjusted the *Opacity* of the March type layer to 32% to make the type very faint, so you can read the text placed across it.

Preparing pictures for e-mail

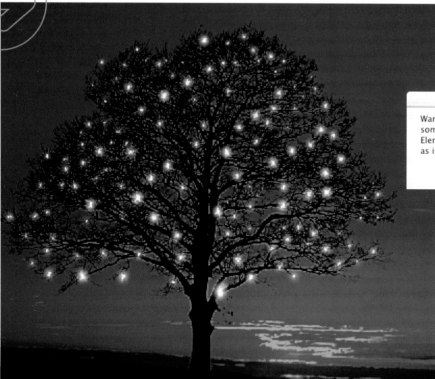

1 Photoshop Elements will do most of the hard work for you at the press of a button. With the original image open, click on the *Attach to E-mail* button in the shortcuts bar or choose *File > Attach to E-mail*.

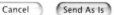

Attach to Email

Warning: The image you are sending may be too large for some recipients to download. Would you like Photoshop Elements to Auto Convert it to a smaller size or send the file as is?

Auto Convert   Cancel   Send As Is

2 If your image is too large, Elements will warn you and give you three options: *Cancel*, *Auto Convert*, or *Send As Is*. If your recipient has broadband Internet access, you may be safe taking the last option. Otherwise, use *Auto Convert* and let Photoshop create a smaller, compressed version. Alternatively, click *Cancel* to make your own optimized image using the *Save for Web* option.

As almost everyone now has access to the Internet and e-mail, sending images to friends or family is now one of the easiest and most direct ways of sharing them. However, this usually requires a little preparation on your part. Not everyone has a fast broadband Internet connection, and large image files can clog up a slower Modem connection for longer than your image's recipient might care for. The trick to sharing images online is to learn how to shrink those file sizes down without adversely affecting image quality.

PREPARING AN IMAGE FOR E-MAIL.
If either you or your recipient has an older computer with a slow 28K modem, then choose a small file size of no more than 200Kb. For a 56K modem you can send file sizes of up to 1Mb, which is large enough for a good-sized print at 200 to 300dpi/ppi. You can send much larger files if you have the time. A broadband modem will let you send professional hi-res documents as long as the recipient has a broadband modem as well. I always keep low-res photos for e-mail in a specific folder, so that when I want to attach an image, I know exactly where I can find it.

3 If your image is OK in size, or you use the *Auto Convert* option, your e-mail application will open automatically and create a new message dialog box. Simply fill in the relevant details. The photograph should already be there as an attachment.

Send Attach Address Fonts Colors Save As Draft

To: Mum & Dad
Cc:
Subject: tree with lights

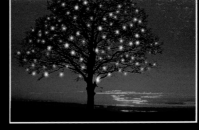

The strength of e-mail is its immediacy. One minute after you've sent your photo, Uncle Jim on the other side of the world can see what you have been up to.

SAVE FOR WEB

File	Edit	Image	Enhance	L

New...   ⌘N
New from Clipboard
Open...   ⌘O
Browse...   ⇧⌘O
Open Recent   ▶

Create Photomerge...

Close   ⌘W
Close All   ⌥⌘W
Save   ⌘S
Save As...   ⇧⌘S
Save for Web...   ⌥⇧⌘S
Revert

Attach to E-mail...
Create Web Photo Gallery...
Online Services...

Place...
Import   ▶
Export   ▶

Batch Processing...

4 If you are preparing images for online use, or you want more control when attaching an e-mail, try the *Save for Web* command. This tool lets you optimize your image for use on the Web, and will create the perfect balance between file size and image quality.

Image	Enhance	Lay

Duplicate Image...
Rotate   ▶
Transform   ▶
Crop
Resize   ▶   Image Size...
Adjustments   ▶   Canvas Size...
                        Reveal All
Histogram...   Scale
Mode   ▶

5 If a dialog box appears saying that the file is too big for optimizing, then use the *Image > Resize > Image Size* command to reduce the size by a suitable amount.

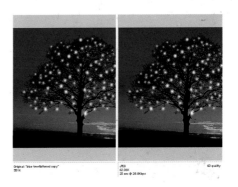

6 A dialog appears, letting you change the size and resolution. For a reasonable file size, choose a size about 5 inches wide and a resolution of 100ppi. Now go back to *File > Save for Web.*

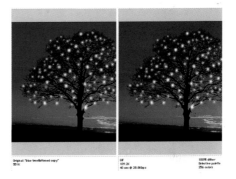

7 Another dialog box appears displaying your original photograph and the optimized version for the Web. You can see the file sizes underneath each version, while the optimized version also shows figures for quality and the time it would take for someone to download the image using a slow 28.8K modem connection.

TIP → Click on *Progressive* to create a small low-res image that is displayed while the full image is downloading. Also, check that the *Constrain Proportions* box is ticked or the image may distort.

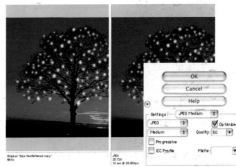

8 Here I have changed the settings from GIF to JPEG Medium with a quality of 60 using the *Custom* button.

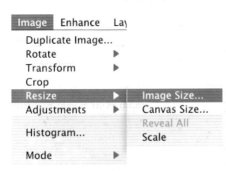

9 The final quality setting of 30 has shrunk a file that was 551Kb in size to a mere 25.72Kb, with a minimal loss of quality.

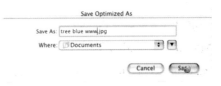

10 To prevent overwriting the original file with a low-res version, you are prompted to save the file in a different place using a different name.

Pictures on the web

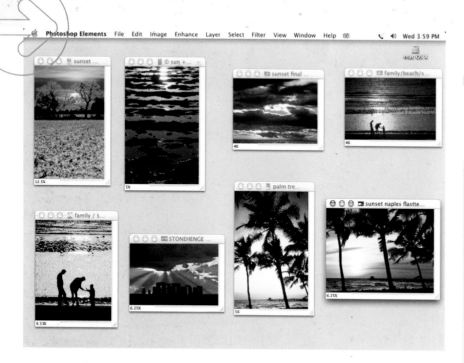

A dobe Photoshop Elements lets you create your own web pages using various design templates. Some are good, some are fun, and some, frankly, are for the kids. This is a great way to get some shots on the Web quickly and easily. Afterward, you can upload the files to your web server or do further work in an application such as Macromedia Dreamworks or Adobe GoLive. This is a powerful tool. Only a few years ago this work would have taken hours, or even days—now Adobe Elements can do it in minutes.

1 This shows the images that I want to turn into web pages. I've collected them all in one folder for ease of use. You can have as many as you like. For speed it is best to create small JPEGs first or the whole process gets quite slow. Use *Image Size* to reduce the file sizes if they are really big. I've just created one folder on the desktop and called it "Sunsets." At this point it is a good idea to create a second folder for the destination files. Create a new folder and call it "Web Browser." This is where you will save all the files you create. If you miss one file, the whole project fails to open, or parts of it are missing when viewing it in your web browser.

TIP On the Internet there is always the chance that someone will copy your work and use it illegally—so beware. In the *Options* drop-down menu there is a copyright option, letting you take measures that will prevent this from happening.

2 Go up to the *Menu Bar* and select *File > Create a Web Photo Gallery*

3 A dialog box opens with quite a lot of boxes to fill. Don't panic! Most of them just contain personal details to be displayed on your website, including your e-mail address and any contact information.

Antique Paper
Bears
Horizontal Dark
Horizontal Frame
Lace
Museum
Office
✓ Simple
Space
Spot Light
Table
Theater
Vacation
Vertical Frame
Wet

4 Click on the *Styles* drop-down menu to choose one of the web-page templates. You may want to try out several designs.

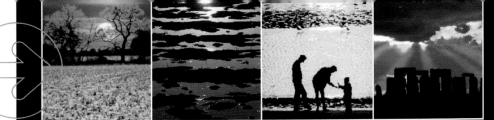

Putting your work on the Web lets potentially thousands of people see it. It is a great marketing tool if you need one.

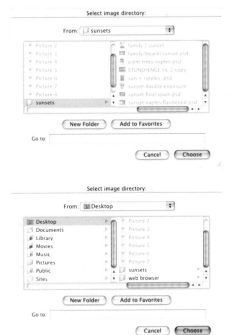

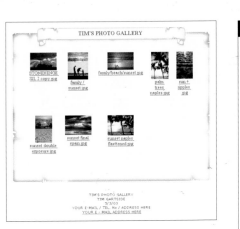

FACT FILE

Alternate template designs
Here, I've used a few more of the template designs. This one is called *Horizontal Dark*. In the *Options* menu for this design you can choose various different sizes for your pictures. The *Pixels* box lets you create your own custom size, if required. The higher the JPEG quality, the bigger the size, the longer each photo will take to open when you click on them while browsing on the Internet. Using your browser to test the speed offline will give a false impression, as there is no time lag when the photo is downloading from the ISP's server.

7 Click *OK* and your web page will be created, along with all of the necessary files, in the target folder. Double-click on it to open it in your browser. This is the antique-paper web page template.

Click on one of the thumbnails and a larger version appears with the same antique-paper design. Your website will now have a slick, professional feel to it, even if it took only ten minutes to produce.

5 Click on *Choose* and a new dialog box opens up to let you navigate to folders elsewhere on your computer. Select *Image Directory*—here I selected the "Sunsets" file on my desktop. Place all folders on your desktop so you don't have too dig deep to find files. I then clicked on "Sunsets" to open the file and make it active and clicked *Choose*.

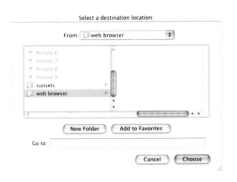

6 Next I selected a destination location, which is where the folder "Web Browser" comes into its own. Select "Web Browser" from the menu and click *Choose*.

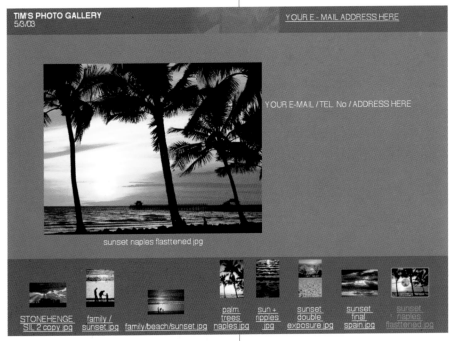

Glossary

aliasing The jagged appearance of diagonal lines in an image, caused by the square shape of pixels.

alpha channel A grayscale version of an image that can be used in conjunction with the other three color channels for storing a mask or selection.

anti-aliasing The smoothing of jagged edges on diagonal lines created in an imaging program, by giving intermediate values to pixels between the steps.

aperture The opening behind the camera lens through which light passes on its way to the CCD.

application Software designed to make the computer perform a specific task. An image-editing program would be an application, as is a word processor.

artifact/artefact A flaw, usually ugly blocks, in a digital image.

ASA American standard for film speed, roughly equivalent to the ISO rating.

aspect ratio The ratio of the height to the width of an image, screen or page.

auto-focus A system used in traditional and digital cameras to ensure that the subject of a photo will be in focus at the moment the exposure is taken.

back-up A copy of a file kept for safety reasons, in case the original becomes damaged or lost. Make back-ups on a regular basis.

bit (binary digit) The smallest data unit of binary computing, being a single 1 or 0. Eight bits make up one byte.

bit-depth The number of bits of color data for each pixel in a digital image. A photographic-quality image needs eight bits for each of the red, green and blue color channels, for a bit-depth of 24.

bitmap An image composed of a grid of pixels, each with their own color and brightness values. When viewed at actual pixel size or less, the image resembles a continuous tone shot, like a photograph.

blend mode A setting in the Photoshop/Photoshop Elements layers palette, which controls how the pixels in one layer affect those in the layers below.

brightness The level of light intensity. One of the three dimensions of color. See also Hue and Saturation

byte Eight bits — the basic data unit of desktop computing. See also bit

calibration The process of adjusting a device, such as a monitor, so that it works consistently with others, such as scanners and printers.

CCD (Charge-Coupled Device) A tiny photocell, made more sensitive by carrying an electrical charge before it is exposed, and used to turn light into an electronic signal. Used in densely packed arrays, CCDs are the recording medium in some scanners and most digital cameras.

CD (Compact Disc) Optical storage medium. As well as the read-only CD-ROM format, used by most computers to install applications, there are two recordable CD formats. On a CD-R (Compact Disc-Recordable), each area of the disc can only be written to once, although it's possible to keep adding data in different "sessions." On a CD-RW (Compact Disc Rewritable) the data can be overwritten many times.

channel Part of an image as stored in the computer; similar to a layer. Commonly, a color image will have a channel allocated to each primary color (e.g. RGB) and sometimes one or more for a mask or other effects. See Alpha Channel

cloning In an image-editing program, the process of duplicating pixels from one part of an image to another, often to cover a fault.

CMOS (Complementary Metal-Oxide Semiconductor) An alternative sensor technology to the CCD, CMOS chips are used in ultra-high resolution cameras from Canon and Kodak.

CMS (Color Management System) Software (sometimes hardware) that ensures color consistency between different devices, so that at all stages of image-editing, from input to output, the color balance stays the same.

CMYK (Cyan, Magenta, Yellow, Key) The four process colors used for printing, including black (key).

compression Technique for reducing the amount of space that a file occupies, through the removal of redundant data.

continuous-tone image An image, such as a photograph, in which there is a smooth progression of tones between black and white.

contrast The range of tones across an image from bright highlights to dark shadows.

cropping The process of removing unwanted areas of an image, leaving behind only the most significant portion.

default The standard setting or action used by an application unless deliberately changed by the user.

depth of field The distance in front of and behind the point of focus in a photograph in which the scene remains in acceptable sharp focus.

dialog An on-screen window in an application, used to enter or adjust settings, or complete a procedure.

diffusion The scattering of light by a material, resulting in a softening of the light and of any shadows cast. Diffusion occurs in nature through mist and cloud-cover, and can also be simulated in professional lighting set-ups using diffusion sheets and soft-boxes.

digital A way of representing any form of information in binary form (ones and zeros). Digital images need large numbers of binary units (bits) to look like continuous-tone photos; when displayed these are in the form of pixels.

dithering A technique used to create an illusion of true-color and continuous tone in situations where only a few colors are actually used. By arranging tiny dots of four or more colors into complex patterns, the printer or display produces an appearance of there being more than 16 million visible colors.

dMax (Maximum Density) The maximum density – that is, the darkest tone – that can be recorded by a device.

dMin (Minimum Density) The minimum density – that is, the brightest tone – that can be recorded by a device.

download Sending a data file from the computer to another device, such as a printer. More commonly, this has come to mean taking a file from the internet or remote server and putting it onto the desktop computer. See also upload

dpi (dots-per-inch) A measure of resolution in half-tone printing. See also ppi

drag Moving an icon or a selected image across the screen, normally by moving the mouse while keeping its button pressed.

dynamic range The range of tones that an imaging device can distinguish, measured as the difference between its dMin and dMax. The dynamic range is affected by the sensitivity of the hardware and by the bit depth.

feathering The fading of the edge of a digital image or selection.

file format The method of writing and storing information (such as an image) in digital form.

fill-in flash A technique that uses the on-camera flash or an external flash in combination with natural or ambient light to reveal detail in the scene and reduce shadows.

filter (1) A thin sheet of transparent material placed over a camera lens to modify the quality of color or light hitting the film or sensor.

filter (2) A feature in an image-editing application that alters or transforms selected pixels for some kind of visual effect.

focal length The distance between the optical center of a lens and its point of focus when the lens is focused on infinity.

focal range The range over which a camera or lens is able to keep a subject in focus (for example, 0.5m to infinity).

focus The optical state where the light rays converge on the film or CCD to produce the sharpest possible image.

fringe A usually-unwanted border effect to a selection, where the pixels combine some of the colors inside the selection and some from the background.

f-stop The calibration of the aperture size of a photographic lens.

GB (gigabyte) Approximately one thousand Megabytes or one billion bytes (actually 1,073,741,824).

graduation The smooth blending of one tone or color into another, or from transparent to colored in a tint. A graduated lens filter, for instance, might be dark on one side, fading to clear at the other.

graphics tablet A flat rectangular board with electronic circuitry that is sensitive to the pressure of a stylus. Connected to a computer, it can be configured to represent the screen area and then be used for drawing.

grayscale An image made up of a sequential series of 256 gray tones, covering the entire gamut between black and white.

GUI (Graphic User Interface) Screen display that uses icons and other graphic means to simplify the use of an application or computer.

handle Icons used in an imaging application to manipulate a picture element. They usually appear on-screen as small black squares.

histogram A map of the distribution of tones in an image, in graph form. The horizontal axis goes from the darkest tones to the lightest, while the vertical axis shows the number of pixels in that range.

hot-shoe An accessory fitting found on most digital and film SLR cameras and some high-end compact models, normally used to control an external flash unit.

HSB (Hue, Saturation and Brightness) The three dimensions of color, and the standard color model used to adjust color in many image-editing applications.

hue The pure color defined by position on the color spectrum; what is generally meant by "color" in lay terms. See also Brightness and Saturation.

image-editing program Software that makes it possible to enhance and alter a digital image.

interpolation A procedure used when resizing a bitmap image to maintain resolution. If the number of pixels is increased beyond those existing in the original image, interpolation creates new pixels to fill in the gaps by comparing the values of adjacent pixels.

ISO An international standard rating for film speed, with the film getting faster as the rating increases. ISO 400 film is twice as fast as ISO 200, and will produce a correct exposure with less light and/or a shorter exposure. However, higher speed film tends to produce more grain in the exposure, too.

JPEG (Joint Photographic Experts Group) Pronounced "jay-peg," a lossy system for compressing images, developed as an industry standard by the International Standards Organization. Compression ratios are typically between 10:1 and 20:1. Higher levels of JPEG compression mean more loss, and therefore a lower quality image.

KB (kilobyte) Approximately one thousand bytes (actually 1,024).

lasso A selection tool used to draw an outline around an area of an image for the purposes of selection.

layer One level of an image file to which objects can be assigned or copied, allowing them to be adjusted and manipulated, without affecting the image as a whole. Layers can be made more or less transparent, their position can be changed within the stacking order, and they can be made visible or invisible, and even deleted, at will.

luminosity The brightness of a color, independent of hue or saturation. Known as Brightness in the HSB color model.

macro A mode offered by specialized lenses and many compact digital cameras that enables the lens or camera to obtain sharp focus on objects in extreme close-up.

mask In image-editing, a grayscale template used to confine alterations to selected parts of an image, protecting the rest.

MB (megabyte) Approximately one thousand kilobytes or one million bytes (actually 1,048,576).

megapixel A rating of resolution for a digital camera, directly related to the number of pixels output by the CMOS or CCD sensor. The higher the megapixel rating, the higher the resolution of images created by the camera.

memory card The storage format used by most digital cameras, where images are saved to solid-state memory chips embedded in a small plastic housing. Common types include Compact Flash, SmartMedia, Memory Stick (Sony), SD Memory Card (Panasonic) and XD Memory Card (Fuji/Olympus).

menu In an application, an on-screen list of choices used to access features or change settings.

microdrive Miniature hard disk designed to fit in the memory-card slot of a digital camera and so increase the storage capacity.

midtone The parts of an image that are approximately average in tone, falling midway between the highlights and shadows.

mode One of a number of alternative operating conditions for a program or tool. For instance, in an image-editing program, RGB color and grayscale are two of the possible modes. Similarly, a selection brush tool may be switchable between selection and mask modes.

noise (1) Random patterns of small spots on a digital image, generally unwanted, and prone to show up in darker areas. Caused by non-image-forming inteference signals in the camera's CCD.

paste Placing a copied image or digital element into an open file. In image-editing programs, this normally takes place in a new layer.

peripheral An external hardware device connected to and operated by the computer, e.g. a printer.

pixel (PICture ELement) The smallest unit of a digitized image — the square screen dots that make up a bitmapped picture. Each pixel carries a specific tone and color.

plug-in Software produced by a third party and intended to supplement a program's performance.

ppi (pixels-per-inch) A measure of resolution for a bitmapped image.

RAM (Random Access Memory) The working memory of a computer, to which the central processing unit (cpu) has direct, immediate access.

RAW A file format created by some high-end digital cameras, containing all the pixel information with no compression. Usually requires proprietary software supplied with the camera to view, adjust and convert the files.

re-sampling Changing the resolution of an image either by removing pixels (lowering resolution) or adding them by interpolation (increasing resolution).

resolution The level of detail in an image, measured in pixels-per-inch (on a monitor) or dots-per-inch (in a printed image, e.g. 1200 dpi).

RGB (Red, Green, Blue) The primary colors of the additive model, as used in monitors and image-editing programs.

saturation The purity of a color, going from the lightest tint to the deepest, most saturated tone. See also Hue and Brightness.

scanner Device that digitizes an image or real object into a bitmapped image. Flatbed scanners accept flat artwork as originals, and can scan transparencies and negatives with the aid of an adaptor. Slide scanners are designed specifically to scan 35mm transparencies and negatives, usually at higher resolutions and bit-depths.

selection A part of the on-screen image that is chosen and defined by a border, in preparation for manipulation or movement.

shutter The mechanical device inside a conventional camera which controls the length of time during which the film is exposed to light. Many digital cameras don't have a shutter as such, but the term is still used as shorthand to describe the electronic mechanism that controls the length of exposure for the CCD.

shutter lag The delay between pressing the shutter release on a digital camera and the exposure being made, caused by the time taken to finalise focus and exposure settings, and the time taken to write the image file to a memory card. The length of this delay was a problem with early digital cameras, but most recent models use a memory buffer to lessen the delay.

shutter speed The time the shutter (or electronic switch) leaves the CCD or film open to light during an exposure, set as fractions of a second (e.g. 1/250).

SLR (Single Lens Reflex) A camera which transmits the same image via a mirror to the film and viewfinder, ensuring that you get exactly what you see in terms of focus and composition.

spot meter A specialized light meter, or function of the camera light meter, that takes an exposure reading for a precise area of a scene. This is particularly useful for ensuring that vital parts of the scene are correctly exposed.

SuperCCD A Fuji-designed CCD in which the photosensors are octagonal in shape and arranged in a tight-packed honeycomb grid. Processing the read-out of each line of pixels requires some interpolation, but this results in images of a higher resolution than the physical pixel count.

telephoto A photographic lens with a long focal length that enables distant objects to be enlarged. The drawbacks include a limited depth of field and angle of view.

thumbnail Miniature on-screen representation of an image file, used for identification and selection of images in a browser window, or to make adjustments in an image-editing application.

TIFF (Tagged Image File Format) A file format for bitmapped images, which can use lossless LZW compression. TIFFs retain more of the original picture information than a JPEG file, and can even store layer information. The most widely used standard for high-resolution digital photographic images once they have been downloaded from the digital camera and edited.

tool A program specifically designed to produce a particular effect on-screen, activated by choosing an icon and using it as the cursor. In image-editing applications, many tools are the equivalents of traditional graphic ones, such as a paintbrush, pencil or airbrush, while others have evolved from techniques used in traditional photographic darkrooms.

toolbar An area of the screen used to provide immediate access to the most frequently used tools, settings and commands.

Upload To transfer a file from a desktop computer onto a network or the internet. For example, you might upload images to a website for use in a Web gallery.

USM (Unsharp Mask) A sharpening technique achieved by combining a slightly blurred negative version of an image with its original positive.

vector graphic A computer image in which the elements are stored as mathematically defined lines, curves, fills and colors. Vector graphics can be scaled up or scaled down at will without any effect on resolution or file size.

white balance A digital camera control used to balance exposure and color settings for artificial lighting types with a different color temperature than daylight.

zoom A camera lens with an adjustable focal length giving, in effect, a range of lenses in one. Drawbacks include a smaller maximum aperture and increased distortion over a prime lens (one with a fixed focal length).

Index

Acknowledgments

Thanks to Alan Buckingham for his help in forming the initial
structure for this book, and for his advice during the early stages
of its writing. Thanks, also, to the editorial and design teams at
Ilex for their work on words and layout.

I would also like to thank Dominique Dallet, for encouragement
and inspiration while I was shooting in Spain. Most of all, thanks
to my wife, Yvonne Gartside, for her support, constructive
criticism and creative input during every stage of this project.

Useful Addresses

Adobe (Photoshop, Illustrator)
www.adobe.com
Agfa www.agfa.com
Alien Skin (Photoshop Plug-ins)
www.alienskin.com
Apple Computer www.apple.com
Association of Photographers (UK)
www.the-aop.org
British Journal of Photography
www.bjphoto.co.uk
Canon www.canon.com
www.powershot.com
Corel (Photo-Paint, Draw, Linux)
www.corel.com
Digital camera information
www.photo.askey.net
Epson www.epson.com
Extensis www.extensis.com
Formac www.formac.com
Fractal www.fractal.com
Fujifilm www.fujifilm.com
Hasselblad www.hasselblad.se
Hewlett-Packard www.hp.com
Iomega www.iomega.com
Kingston (memory) www.kingston.com
Kodak www.kodak.com
LaCie www.lacie.com
Lexmark www.lexmark.com
Linotype www.linotype.org
Luminos (paper and processes)
www.luminos.com

Macromedia
www.macromedia.com
Microsoft www.microsoft.com
Minolta www.minolta.com
www.minoltausa.com
Nikon www.nikon.com
Nixvue www.nixvue.com
Olympus
www.olympusamerica.com
Paintshop Pro www.jasc.com
Pantone www.pantone.com
Philips www.philips.com
Photographic information site
www.ephotozine.com
Photoshop tutorial sites
www.planetphotoshop.com
www.ultimate-photoshop.com
Polaroid www.polaroid.com
Qimage Pro
www.ddisoftware.com/qimage/
Ricoh www.ricoh-usa.com
Samsung www.samsung.com
Sanyo www.sanyo.co.jp
Shutterfly (Digital Prints via the web)
www.shutterfly.com
Sony www.sony.com
Sun Microsystems www.sun.com
Symantec www.symantec.com
Umax www.umax.com
Wacom (graphics tablets)
www.wacom.com